Published in the United States by Vendere Consulting

FIRST EDITION

ISBN: 0999427717
ISBN 9780999427712
Library of Congress Control Number: 2017918834
Vendere Consulting, Raleigh, NC

Table of Contents

Introduction

I believe that sales is a noble profession.

As critical as every function in a company is, it all starts with an order from a customer. The revenue from that order pays for the engineering that designs the product, the manufacturing teams that get it built, logistics teams that get it to the customer, and all of the back-office functions that make sure that the company keeps running well.

All of these functions are equally important to taking care of the customer and earning a profit for the shareholders, but it all has to start with an order that a salesperson has won.

For such a critical role and process, it is shocking how little serious attention salespeople get in most organizations. When I say "attention," I'm not talking about visibility. Salespeople are always visible, particularly when they are missing their numbers.

What I mean by attention—serious attention—is having a management structure that looks at the salespeople and keeps them in the same state of continuous improvement as any process in the company.

In many companies, the attention is on numbers and results for a short, recent time period. Sales managers in these companies spend their time staring at spreadsheets and business-intelligence dashboards looking for gaps in performance and delivering the standard "Row harder!" messaging when gaps are detected.

If you took the time to pick up this book and read this far, I would wager that it's how your company is running things.

Those "Row harder!" messages have always been a sore point for me. When a sales team is coming up short, the problem is almost never about desire.

Have you ever met a good salesperson who does not know right where he or she is in relation to quota for the period? Have you ever met a good salesperson who does not want to make his or her number? Good salespeople don't need their managers to tell them where they stand. Good salespeople don't need their managers to tell them to work harder.

Good salespeople need their managers to help them focus on the right activities to ensure that they meet their quotas.

The best sales managers whom I have met think like investment bankers. These sales managers think about return on investment in terms of the real currency that they have to spend—hours of their salespeople's time.

What do the sales managers focus on instead? Their managers. Far too much of a sales manager's role today has become about reporting up in the organization about what is going on rather than about the work needed to make things better.

This is not a book about selling; plenty has been written on this by authors far more gifted than I am. This is a book about sales management. The subtitle of this book is not suggested lightly. For all of the reasons that we discuss above, most sales managers are simply not focused on helping their salespeople to perform better.

Humor me for a moment while I tell you a story.

Back when I was just starting out, I worked for a great sales manager named Bill Hughes. Bill was a trim man with white hair and bright eyes that always gleamed a bit behind his glasses. Bill had started out in the manufacturing plant and worked his way into sales with a pragmatic understanding of just what it took to keep the business running and take care of customers.

I was just a couple of years into the game when my annual review was coming up, and I was facing a miss to my quota for the first time in my career. I was nervous about it, and it showed. I stumbled my way through the first part of the review, and Bill finally had to stop it and ask me what the heck was going on.

"Bill, I'm nervous that you are about to fire me."

"Why in the world would you think that?"

"Because I am about to miss my number for the year."

"So?"

"Well, the last time that I checked, that was bad."

"Let me ask you a question: Have you done everything that I have told you to do?"

"Yes."

"Did you do it well?"

"I think so, but that doesn't matter; I did not get the result."

> "Look, there are only a few reasons for you to not make your number. Either you did not do what I told you to do, you did not do it well, or I told you to do the wrong thing. If you did what I told you to do and did it well, then it's my fault that you did not make your number. I told you to do the wrong things—and it's my job to help you fix that."

I have never forgotten that conversation—and I never missed my number again after that. When it became my turn to lead other salespeople, I made it a point to follow the same philosophy about the role and fundamental responsibility of sales managers: helping their salespeople to make their number.

Sadly, as I have looked around the business world over the years, I have seen far too few examples of this kind of sales management. Don't get me wrong—I don't think that this is a result of the intentions of the sales managers; I think that this is a result of how companies are thinking about their sales teams.

Take a moment now to think about your sales team. How would you answer these questions?

> Do you have the right people on your team now? Are you setting yourself up to ensure that you will continue to?

> Are you building a culture to continuously coach and improve those people?

> Do you have your people in the places where they have the most opportunities to succeed?

> Are you focusing your people on the best customers to get results?

> Do you have your channels in the best deployment to act as a force multiplier for your team?

Do you have a plan for every account that is being executed by your salespeople?

Are your sales calls planned and followed up on?

Is your pipeline being managed properly?

Are your deals moving forward faster than they are for your competition?

And, most importantly, does your team have focus?

If your answer is no to any of them, then you have some fundamental problems.

This is a book about how to fix that. We are going to give detailed solutions that will allow sales managers to help their salespeople focus on the activities and deals that are best going to get results and make their numbers.

For the sales manager, this is going to revolve around three key dimensions: people, place, and process. This is like a three-legged stool; you need to address each of them to really help your team. It all comes down to the people whom you pick for the sales roles, the places that you send them, and the process that you use to help them perform.

Some of the tools that we discuss are more applicable to large companies that have the resources and funding for the kind of data systems that they require. However, no matter how large your sales team or company is, the concepts that these tools address are still going to apply.

The same thing goes for you—the person taking the time to read and think about this book. While it might seem at times that the concepts here only apply at the sales-vice-president level, that is not the intent. The real target of my message is where the rubber meets the road: the frontline sales manager leading a team of salespeople.

Regardless of the level on which you fall on the spectrum of sales leadership, you can be part of the solution that will help us offer better leadership to our salespeople.

Depending on your level of experience, you may already have well-developed approaches around people and place. If that is the case, then you may want to focus on chapter three. This section of the book represents some fundamentally new concepts that combine predictive analytics with customer-relationship management (CRM) software.

Far too often the salesperson feels like they are the servant of the CRM software, instead of the other way around. These concepts let you put your CRM to work for the salesperson, delivering insights that help the salesperson to focus their time on the most important things.

As you dive into the book, don't feel obligated to drill into all the details of the tools presented. Some of them get fairly complex. Think more about the core ideas and then the details. The details only matter if I can convince you that this approach to sales management will make a difference for you.

It has certainly made a difference for me.

Chapter 1

People

Let me tell you a story about one of the first big "people" lessons that I learned as a sales manager. It was the first time that I really had to face the fundamental difference between a true salesperson and a person who is just there to transact business.

> I was building up a sales team in Los Angeles and had inherited some people from some prior sales teams. LA had been one of those puzzling cities where we had never been able to get our business built out to the level that we expected, so we were going to try to mix things up with some new resources. One of the new salespeople was a guy named Mick.
>
> Mick was a nice, easygoing guy. He was shaggy haired and a bit rumpled, but he was professional and knowledgeable of both the market and the technology that we were selling.
>
> Mick had been around the business for years, primarily as what we called a price negotiator. When a salesperson was working on a deal, he or she would work with the negotiator to get approval for the price that would be quoted to the customer.

This is a critical role in any company as the price negotiators become the guardians of profit. However, as you might imagine from all of the detail required, the burnout factor on the role is pretty high. People would typically rotate out of it into other roles every few years.

Mick reached the point where he really wanted to rotate out, and he ended up on my team. I had never seen Mick sell, but he had been a salesman before, so when his manager offered him to me, I made the assumption that he had the basic chops. It was also not going to hurt me to do a favor for his boss.

Mick came into the team easily since he already knew all of the other members and was familiar with the product, its applications, and the customer base. We had the normal conversations to set up target customers and a go-to-market plan, and I set Mick loose to see what he could do.

After a couple of months with normal coaching conversations, it was clear that things were just not getting moving for him, so I went down to LA to dive a bit deeper with Mick and figure out where the gaps were and what we could best do for a course correction.

We talked through his customer list and the status of all of his channel partners. It was puzzling. On paper, everything looked like Mick was set up for success.

We were starting to brainstorm a bit on other approaches that we could take when Mick said something that just stopped me dead in my tracks: "I don't know what it is, Charles. I come into the office every day and sit here at my desk, but the phone is just not ringing."

Wow. Just wow.

That happened twenty years ago, and it was such a stark moment that I can still remember it like it was yesterday. In the span of just a few seconds, Mick told me with the force of a sledgehammer that as nice a guy as he is, he was not in any way a true salesperson.

In this chapter, we are going to talk about how to avoid the conversation above from ever happening in the first place. The focus on people will be about how to identify the true salespeople in your organization, how to coach them to thrive, and how to hire the right people going forward.

How many times do you think that this scenario has played out? A group of managers is sitting in a room doing a personnel review. They come across a guy like Mick—someone who is nice, experienced, and well thought of but is just not in the right job. They can't think of a good spot for him, so they default to giving him a try in sales.

This has and does happen far too often. Why? Fundamentally, most people don't understand what the art and profession of selling really is. Some people's opinions are skewed by the classic stereotypes of the used-car salesman, but I believe that most people confuse selling with a pure process. If you do steps A and B, you will get result C.

I want to be careful here with how we are defining things so that we don't get into a huge semantic debate. The functional act of transacting a sale is not what I am talking about when I talk about "selling" in this book. While it is a necessary and critical function, transacting a sale is not selling.

The kind of selling that we are going to talk about in this book is consultative-demand creation. In its most perfect form, this level of selling has salespeople work with customers to see problems that they may not even know that they have and then command value for solving them.

Selling at that level is hard. Very hard. It takes deep domain knowledge paired with exceptional listening and communication skills. It's part science and part art, and it takes years of experience to become competent at it.

However, before you can even get to that point, you have to start with the right person. This runs us smack into the classic "nature versus nurture" question. After years of working with many, many salespeople, I've come for the firm belief that to be a true salesperson, you have to be wired a certain way in the first place.

Let's play with an analogy for a moment: golf.

I love golf. I've played it for years and invested far more time, money, and effort into it than I would ever be comfortable admitting. Nobody who knows me well can deny that I have been dedicated in my practice and have had the advantage of some truly gifted coaches, trainers, and playing partners.

With all of this, I can assure you—and anyone who has ever played with me can back this up—I suck at it.

I really, really suck at it. I'm not taking about not being particularly poor at it; I am talking about a "Cover your eyes; you don't want to see this" level of bad.

Why?

All in all, I have the hand-eye coordination of a rock.

I'm simply not wired to play golf well.

To take on any activity, all the training and determination in the world does not matter if you don't have the basic capabilities to do it in the first place. It's one of the reasons that there are very few starting centers in the NBA who are under five feet tall.

Sales is no different. While coaching and training can make someone a better salesperson, there are characteristics that you have to be born with to be able to do the job in the first place.

We will start this section of the book by looking at how to objectively view your team and really understand your current state. We will go deeper into just which attributes make up a "true salesperson" and how to detect those attributes in both your existing team members and any new hires that you bring in.

The next part of the section is about coaching. Once you know that you have people who are wired as true salespeople, how can you best work with them to help them be more effective than if they were just out there running on their own? How can you best improve the performance of team members when conventional coaching does not get the job done?

We finish by talking about how to structure your management of the sales team and the support teams around it to actually help the salespeople to be more effective and get in front of their customers more. This is probably one of the most important things that a sales manager can do to help his or her team.

Chapter 1-1

Assessing the State of Your Team

Whether you are taking over a new team or just trying to get a new perspective on an existing one, there is real value to taking a systematic approach to get the most objective view possible.

> I'd been brought in to turn around an existing sales team. It had a mature product line, lots of long-service employees, and declining sales over a number of years. I'd made a deal with the leadership to give me ninety days to meet the team and figure out the current state before we pushed the buttons on any changes.
>
> I did not know any of the people on the team or have any relationships with the organization, so the evaluation was going to be as objective as possible.
>
> For the first ninety days, I did just that with the core team. First, I met with all of the managers and got their rundowns, person by person, on their teams. I kept the same structure to the questions so that I had a consistent view from person to person:
>
> * Is he or she a hunter or farmer?
> * Using school grades of A to F, how good is the person at selling?

* Who are the person's major customers?
* What were the person's last sales results?
* What does this person need improvement on?
* Do you want to keep this person or move him or her out?

It's fairly blunt, but that's what you need, particularly on the last question. The team had been missing its results for years. Even though there were more issues than just the sales team in that business, you really had to question any managers who tried to give an overly rosy picture of their teams.

Then came the hard work: hour-long, one-to-one interviews with all of the salespeople to gauge them for myself and to get their views of what was going on with the business. These were set up around regional staff meetings that the managers held while we pulled the salespeople out one by one for the interviews.

After ninety days, I set up a meeting with leadership to review the results, and my boss had me go to lunch with him just before the meeting to get a preview. We set off in his car to his favorite Mexican joint when he came right to the point:

"So, how bad is it?"

"Well, I can give you the answer a couple of ways. Do you want to know how many people we need to absolutely get rid of, or do you want to know how many I would hire off the street if they were actually new candidates?"

"Oh, it has to be how many would you hire. That has to be the standard to hold ourselves to. What would that be?"

"A third."

"We need to get rid of a third of the salesforce?"

"No, I would only keep a third of the salespeople that we have today."

That was when his head exploded.

Was that a brutal assessment? Absolutely, but the goal here had been to find the true salespeople. The team sold a highly technical product, and its ranks had been recruited primarily from engineers. Every single one of them was technically competent and professional. Almost all of them were diligent and hard working. There were just too many of them who simply were not true salespeople. That basic root issue—and the culture that it tied to—led to all kinds of related problems with this sales team that were going to have to be fixed before any real improvement would be seen.

If you are reading this book, chances are that you are either in the process of taking over a team or have a team that you know you need to do something different with. Regardless of which of these two categories you fit into, the first thing that you need to do is to make the same kind of brutally honest and objective assessment of both your sales team and the environment in which they are working. Only then can you work out a realistic strategy and plan for improvement that goes beyond just "Row harder!"

The starting point for this is a method that I learned from a man named Andy Gravitt. Andy is hands down the best leader under whom I have ever had the privilege to work. To a person, everyone I know who has worked for Andy considers him the best boss that he or she ever had.

When Andy came in to take over our division, the first thing he did was to set up meetings with every single team, during which the team members presented what they did, where they were going, what issues they were facing, and what help they needed.

Andy waited until he had gone through all of those meetings and had reflected on what he saw before he ever said a word about the new strategy that he wanted to follow and where he thought we should go with the business.

All the people in the organization felt like they had some real input into the ultimate strategy. Whether or not their specific issues were part of the final plan, they knew that they had at least been listened to, and that drove real buy-in to the new plan.

The same principle applies to the specific case of taking a sales team to the next level. In this chapter, we will lay out a structure that you can use to make that happen.

For the purposes of a sales team, you need to start by looking at four key areas: the sales-team members themselves, the channel that they are working with, the offer that they have to sell, and the marketing that is driving demand for that offer.

This is by no means meant to be an exhaustive review of those four areas. By design, we want to focus just on how the activities and functions in these areas are impacting the effectiveness of the sales force.

In each of the four areas, you will start with some metrics that you will gather from your finance team. There may be other metrics that you want to look at, but I have listed the most important ones along with what they should tell you.

After you have all of the numbers straight, you need to get out on a "listening tour," meeting as many of your salespeople as possible, along with your channel partners and any customers that make sense.

You are looking to understand how the world looks through their eyes. Your watchword on this tour should be *empathy.* At this point you have no real idea of what the core issues are, and you just want to learn, as objectively as possible, what they are all seeing.

The Sales Team

This is the longest part of the process. We have a lot of things to look at with any sales team, starting with the numbers. Numbers don't tell the whole story, but they are the best starting point as long as you understand what to look for behind them later. You should have the numbers part done before you start your listening tour to help you to have some context as you meet people.

Depending on the size of your company and the particular systems that you have in place, you may have challenges in getting your hands on as much detailed data as you might like. You might not be able to get all of these numbers, and you might not be able to get the level of granularity that you might like, but you should at least be able to get some of them. Work with what you have so that you are at least bringing some objective measures into your analysis.

These are the key numbers that I like to look at and what they mean in the analysis:

Percentage of salespeople who made plan in the previous period
This is the single most objective measure of the health of an overall sales team. If the numbers show that most of the group is making plan (80 percent or more), then you are in a very healthy position. If most of the group is missing plan (fewer than 50 percent of salespeople making it), then you know you have a major problem.

One special case to be on the lookout for is if a group is making its numbers overall but only due to the efforts of a small cadre of top performers. This means that you have a large population of mediocre-to-poor performers that have to be dealt with. Deal with it you must, as nothing is more demoralizing to a top salesperson as watching mediocre-to-poor salespeople continue to be treated the same as they are.

Percentage of salespeople who had positive growth in the previous period
The only issue with the previous measure is that it does not take the quota-setting process into account. If the quota-setting process

was broken, that statistic can give you a distorted view of your team. Looking at how many folks were able to at least grow their business is a good offset to this and will also tell you if there is an issue with how quotas are being set.

If most people are growing their business but also missing their plans, you not only may have a broken quota-setting process, but you are also setting yourself up for a major morale problem with your sales team. While the mediocre people may not do anything about that, the best salespeople always have options and will be looking into them whenever they feel that they are not being appreciated or fairly measured.

Ratio of salespeople to managers

If sales managers are going to truly coach their salespeople, then they need small-enough teams to have the bandwidth to do meaningful coaching. My experience has been that once the number of direct reports gets to be higher than ten people, the ability of the manager to coach the team starts to decline quickly. Once the number is over fifteen, it is almost nonexistent, and the only thing that the manager can really do is administrative management and crisis response.

Percentage of manager time spent in structured coaching with sales team

Coaching is the single most important thing that sales managers do. At least 10 to 20 percent of their time should be spent on structured coaching. You will probably not be able to find this number in any system, but you can get a sense of this by just asking managers how much time in a given week is scheduled coaching time with their team. (This is discussed in detail in chapter 1-4.)

Number of sales calls made per week

There is no absolute right number for sales calls, as the answer is going to depend heavily on the geography of a territory and the type of sales calls being made. For cold calling and quick-hit encounters, the number should be quite high. For complex consultative selling, it can be just a few per week.

The real trick for this metric is deciding what number you should reasonably expect for your circumstances and then driving actions around it if it is too low. If it is too low, you have to ask yourself what other activities are keeping your sales team from making the number of sales calls that you need. Chances are that those activities could and should be done by other, more appropriate, and less expensive resources in your organization.

Percentage of deals closed last period
Hit rates can vary dramatically from business to business, so you will need to decide what is really the right number for yours. One way to figure out a baseline for your business is to look at the average closure rate for your top salespeople versus your worst ones.

As a general rule, one in ten indicates a relatively weak team, and one in three is a pretty strong one.

Average age of won deals
This number is going to help you to set an age at which managers should reasonably question whether a deal is still viable and should stay in the pipeline, consuming selling time and resources.

An average is just that, so it is not an absolute rule, but it can go a long way toward helping you to clean out the noise from your pipeline. (We will discuss scrubbing the pipeline in more detail in chapter 3-2.)

Average age of deals in overall pipeline
When compared with the average age of won deals, this number can help you to gauge the overall cleanliness of your pipeline.

If the average age of deals in the pipeline is significantly higher than the average age of won deals, then you know that you need to get to work cleaning out deals that are simply not viable.

Percentage of direct vs. indirect accounts

This is not so much an indicator of health as a means of understanding the nature of how you are going to market. Some businesses use channels almost exclusively to service their customers, while others use none at all; either of these models—or the more common mixture of the two—is perfectly fine as long as it matches your intended go-to-market strategy.

If you have a mix of direct and indirect accounts, you will need to be careful to ensure that the salesperson's time is balanced appropriately. In the case of direct accounts, you want to watch out for salespeople spending too much of their time on customer-service issues that other parts of the organization could be handling more effectively.

In the case of indirect accounts, you want to watch out for salespeople becoming secondary to the channel's-sales team and not really driving business forward themselves. (This is discussed in more detail in chapter 2-8 on working with channel partners.)

Number of customers "lost" in the previous period and the total revenue tied to them

I call this the "leaky-bucket metric." Any sales organization is always losing customers. The big ones we almost always know about and, good or bad, we know the reasons why we lost them.

The more insidious impact of the leaky bucket comes from the small customers who just stop buying from us and whom we never hear about. If that number gets high enough, you need one heck of a new-customer pipeline to replace the volume.

When you look at this, don't get too hung up on the definition of a "lost customer." I've seen all kinds of complex definitions used, and they can easily lead to gaming of the metric. Keep it simple. If a customer bought something two periods back but not one period back, call them lost.

One special case is if your customers do a lot of project-based business that does not repeat regularly. If that is the case, then pick a longer period during which you would normally expect to win at least one project, and use that longer period of for your measurement.

In all of these metrics, while the absolute numbers may tell you something specific, the real meaning comes in how they are varying over time. Seeing how the numbers are trending is going to help you prioritize your problems. Going forward, these trends will tell you if your actions are moving your business in the right direction or if you have to take another path to turn them around.

Unfortunately, many of the popular CRMs give you just an instantaneous view of your data and do not keep a historical view of it to allow you to see those trends. Depending on the CRM that you use, you may either need to keep track of the key metrics manually or work with a third-party business-intelligence product that includes a historian, such as Alpine Metrics.

Sales teams are more than just numbers, so this is just a starting point in your analysis; the real meat of it has to come from conducting a listening tour with your team. The details of how you will do this will depend on the structure of the team and the geography that you are dealing with, but in general, the idea is to meet with logical subsets of your team, speaking with the manager and the team members one-on-one and conducting some kind of a town hall. In all of those activities, you will both be asking questions and opening yourself up to questions from the team in both individual and group sessions.

Start with the managers; have them give you basic presentations on their regions and teams. I can't emphasize the importance of this first meeting enough. It's normally assumed that an underperforming team is made up of weak salespeople. This is not automatically the case. More often than not, I have found the root cause to be sales managers who have limited skills or training in coaching and leading a team. Taking a hard look at your management team is only fair to the salespeople whom you are going to be evaluating at the same time.

These presentations from the manager should not be *War and Peace* PowerPoint decks but rather concise overviews of their territories and how they are running them. I normally like to give a template to ensure that it does not turn into a nightmare of what I like to call "PowerPoint vomit." A case can also be made for leaving the structure to the manager as a test of his or her ability to tell the story properly.

During these overview meetings, keep detailed notes. When you compare these presentations to your own impressions of the salespeople and the answers that you got from them in your one-on-one meetings, you will have another measure of the manager.

In any case, you want to follow a flow such as the one below and ask probing questions:

The Organization

This is normally just an org chart, but it can still be a lengthy conversation as you delve into the reasoning behind the structure and commentary is made about different individuals.

Probing Questions:

* Why is the organization structured the way that it is?
* Does the span of control of each manager make sense, and can he or she defend it?
* Who are the top and the bottom salespeople?

* What is being done to ensure that the top people are not flight risks?
* What is being done to improve the performance of—or to exit—the bottom people?

What you are looking for:

* You want to see a reasoned structure to the organization that emphasizes a focus of activity for each of the salespeople.
* You want to see that the managers are able to give objective and fair assessments of their people along with clear plans for what they are doing with them. For example, how did they determine who their top and bottom salespeople were?

Red Flags:

* If the structure is management heavy, there can be an efficiency issue. You want as many resources selling as possible.
* Span of control is ideally about ten people per manager. If the number is much more than that, it is hard for managers to adequately coach their people. If the number is much smaller, there are going to be efficiency issues in your organization.
* The only exception to this rule for me is the "working manager" who carries a personal account load along with coaching three to four salespeople. Working managers can be a great way to establish a bench of future managers, testing out their abilities to lead while having the safety net of a relatively controlled environment.

The Customers and Market in the Region

This is normally a map with slides included to describe how customers and the market lay out within it.

Probing Questions:

* Who are the top five to ten customers?
* What do they do?
* What do they buy from you?
* What do they use the product for?
* What are the states of your relationships with them?
* How have their sales been trending?
* What are the particular demographics of the area that impact your market?
* What are the opportunities for growth in the market?
* What are the headwinds that you could be facing in the market?

What you are looking for:

* Does the manager know the top customers well enough to talk of them in some depth?
* Does the manager have a strategic vision for the region?

Red Flags:

* If it is clear that the manager does not have a relationship with the top customers, that can be a real issue. There are reasons (such as a short tenure in the role) that may well excuse this, but if the manager has been in place for a while, he or she should know the top customers well and have a clear plan for them with salespeople.

* If the thinking for the region is more tactical than strategic, you could have your sales team being too reactive in their activities. To get real growth, you need a sales leader who rises above the day-to-day whirlwind to show the sales team members where they can go to get new business.

The Channels

If you work with channel partners—be they distributors, resellers, or sales representatives—you want to get a good understanding of how they are performing and how well your team is engaging with them.

Probing Questions:

* Who are the top five to ten channel partners?
* What markets do they focus on?
* How have their sales been trending?
* What issues are we having?
* What other lines do they carry?
* What operating rhythm do you use to review performance with the channel partners?

What you are looking for:

* Does the manager know the top channel partners well?
* Is there a culture of collaboration and teamwork between your sales team and the channel partners?
* Does the manager have a plan for improving performance in the future?

Red Flags:

* As with the top customers, the manager should know the top channel partners intimately. If he or she doesn't, you

run the risk of the channel running the region instead of your team.

* The manager needs to be on top of the performance of the channel partners and know precisely why sales performance is up or down. There should be a plan of action running on any channel partner in which the sales performance has been trending down. You want to see that there is a culture of accountability in place and that it runs both ways.
* You really want to take a measure of the nature of the relationships. If they are not fully collaborative, then the team is probably not getting the most out of the partnerships. There are two extremes here, ranging from having the team bossing the channel around to having the channel partners just doing whatever they want. Both are bad. The most effective channel relationships are collaborative and beneficial to both parties.

The Business

Your understanding of how the overall business is working is not really going to come from any specific part of the presentations but from questions that you will ask managers during and at the conclusion of the presentations—unless you want to request specific slides on them. I've done it both ways and tend to prefer asking the questions in the moment to avoid getting too many pat answers.

Probing Questions:

* What does marketing do best? Why?
* What could marketing do better for you? Why?
* What is the best part of our offer? Why?
* What is the one thing that you would want in the offer that you don't have today? Why?
* What part of the business helps you the most? Why?
* What part of the business hinders you the most? Why?

What you are looking for:

* Does the manager see the big picture of the business?
* Does the manager have vision that can contribute to the overall business strategy?

Red Flags:

* One real measure of the potential for advancement of any manager is how strategically he or she is able to look at the business. If all you hear around these issues is a myopic and tactical view, then you don't really have a leader in place; you have more of an administrator. You certainly should expect the managers to see and know all of the tactical issues that they are facing—that is the front-line part of the job—but real leaders also have the ability to see how those issues fit into the larger business and its strategies.

After you have met with the manager, you need to meet with the salespeople one-on-one. In a perfect world, you would have time to meet with each and every salesperson, but if the organization is substantial, just getting a representative sample is going to tell you a lot about both the state of your sales team as well as how the business is really working.

One of the first things that you want to do is to get a sense of the makeup of your sales team. On a broad level, salespeople tend to fall into one of two types: hunters and farmers.

Hunters love to go out after new customers and win the first deal and are less interested in managing the same customers over a long period of time.

Farmers love to take an existing set of customers and get the most possible revenue from them and are less interested in targeting new ones.

Many sales organizations tend to glorify the hunters and denigrate the farmers, but I would argue that this is a simplistic view. There are specific combinations of attributes that make up both of these types of salespeople, and both are critical to having a healthy sales team. The trick is to make sure that you have your salespeople aligned with account packages that match their types. We will talk more about this in chapter 2-2.

In chapter 1-3, we will give a detailed look at an in-depth interview that takes sixty to ninety minutes to do and lets you classify and understand the competency levels of each salesperson. If you really want to get to know your sales team deeply, I highly recommend that you conduct this interview with each salesperson on your listening tour.

If you are moving fast and only have a few minutes to spend with the salespeople, here is a quick but effective set of questions that you can do to get a sense of the issues above:

Basic Questions:

* Tell me a bit about your background. Where did you grow up? Where did you go to school?
* Tell me the story of how you came to take your first job in sales.
* We know your official job description, but in your own words, what do you do?
* To whom in the organization do you most often turn for help? What kind of help?

* What motivates you most as a salesperson?
* I've taken a look at your most recent sales data. What can you tell me about why it is up/down?
* If you could change any one thing at the company—but only one thing—what would you want to change?

What you are looking for:

* Can your salespeople tell clear, concise, compelling stories?
* Do the salespeople have a clear sense of their mission and how to get the job done?
* Do you see a team that can get the job done for you?
* Did you see any potential future managers in the mix?
* Are the top performers secure, or are they possible flight risks?

Red Flags:

* If salespeople can't clearly explain why their sales are where they are and what they are doing to grow or recover them, you need to take a much deeper look. Are there issues with the competence of that salesperson? Is this indicating coaching or leadership issues with the manager? If there are just a few outliers, there are likely just issues with the salesperson, but if you see a wider pattern, it's more probable that there are issues with the manager.
* If the population of weak-to-bad salespeople is too large, you need to expedite doing a deep dive on them to determine what personnel moves you need to make—with both the salespeople and the managers.

Whatever questions you decide to ask, keep detailed notes as you progress on the tour. This is going to serve two very important purposes for you.

First, no matter how well you try to keep things straight in your head, it's too easy to let them mush together or let your own preconceived ideas color the data.

Secondly, when the people whom you are interviewing see that you are taking the trouble to keep detailed notes, they see that you are invested in and value what they are telling you. This will have a big impact later when you need their buy ins on your ultimate strategy.

After you have spoken to all of the managers and salespeople, you need to think about some big overall questions that you can only answer from thinking about all of your observations.

> What is the morale like? Is there a culture of winning, or is missing quota considered routine?
>
> What is the process like? Is there focus and rigor in execution? Are the tools designed to help the salesperson first and foremost?
>
> What is the deployment like? Does it match the opportunities that you want to pursue?

These questions are going to set the priorities for you as you build your strategy.

Answers from your one-on-one meetings to pay particular attention to are the ones from what I like to call the "magic-wand question." Consolidate the results from the question "If you could change any one thing at the company—but only one thing—what would you want to change?" There are going to be some common answers or themes. The ones that come up the most should create an immediate priority list for you as these are the things that, regardless of everything else, your salespeople see as being the most important.

Once you are done with the tour, there is immense value in sending a summary communication out to the team on what you found with that question, along with your commitment to fixing them. Take the top three items, and set an action plan with dates and accountable people for each of them in your communication. As they are handled, communicate to the team just what was done, and thank them again for their input.

If you are getting traction from this activity with your team, you might want to create a perpetual list of top-three issues that is always being worked. As long as you let your sales team know that you are attacking those issues, they will pay you back with an even deeper engagement on their part. Remember, it can get awfully lonely when salespeople are out in the field facing customers. Knowing that their leadership is actively looking to make things better goes a very long way.

Regardless of the strategy you elect after you finish assessing your sales team, it should include tools that help the salespeople drive execution. This will let you create positive morale to drive a culture of winning.

Marketing

It never ceases to amaze me how rarely there is true synergy between sales and marketing. Far too often, when we look at the two groups in a company, they see each other as necessary evils rather than valued partners.

How can you tell how well the sales team is working with marketing? One strong indicator can be how much growth is coming from existing customers versus new customers. This is one of the cleanest measures that we can make of how much genuinely new demand is being created. Taking a quick look at that metric will tell you how well your sales and marketing teams are working together to open new doors.

I've seen a lot of additional ways to measure marketing teams and their campaigns, and, to be perfectly frank, most of the systems that I have seen obfuscate the core metric—are the marketing activities driving new leads, and are those leads generating new business? The challenge that I have with these measurement systems is that they often are based on tying the marketing activities directly to revenue.

The problem with that tie is that it's not really a pure relationship. By the time you realize revenue from a lead or a campaign, you are mixing in the efforts and effectiveness of both the salespeople and the channel. If you really want to tie in revenue, you can, but I would strongly encourage you to make it at most a secondary measurement. To really measure marketing, you have to look at the most direct output that it creates: leads.

When you look at leads, you should look at both the number and the quality of them. The number is easy enough to measure, and the quality can be determined by how far those leads make it down the sales funnel. We will discuss leads in much greater depth in chapter 2-4, but the basic metrics to look at are as follows:

Number of new leads per week
This is the rawest number that you can look at regarding how many leads you have coming in. Even if most of them are garbage, you at least know that they are coming in, and watching this trend over time shows you whether the presence that you are creating is increasing or decreasing.

Percentage of leads that turn into sales calls
This is the first cut of the quality of the leads. If they don't turn into sales calls, then either the qualification team and process have issues, or the leads themselves are weak.

Percentage of leads that turn into opportunities
If the lead was good enough to qualify as a sales call, then the next step beyond that is an opportunity to actually win the business. This does start to also mix in a measure of the sales team's effectiveness, so

this may be as far down the chain as you want to go. If you decide to keep going, the next step would be to measure the percentage of leads that turn into revenue.

It may be impossible to get all of the information in time, but in a perfect world, you would want to have the above numbers as well as feedback from your listening tour with your sales team before you meet with the marketing team.

When you do sit down with your marketing team, it's another step on your listening tour, and there are some probing questions that you should be asking:

Basic questions:

* What do you honestly think of the sales team?
* Tell me about the last time you went on a customer visit with a salesperson. What came out of the visit?
* Which campaigns from the last period generated the most leads? Why do you think that they were so effective?
* Of all the tools that you have developed, which one do you think adds the most value to the salesperson in the field? Why?
* If you could get funding for just one project for the next period, what would it be? Why?

What you are looking for:

* Is there a solid relationship between sales and marketing?
* Do the activities and budget spend align with lead generation for the sales team and channel as a priority?
* Is there a toolbox or library of collateral with truly compelling value propositions for the sales team to work with?

Red Flags:

* Any animosity or lack of mutual respect between the teams is a major red flag. Neither sales nor marketing can be effective without each other.
* Poor alignment between the marketing spend and the sales strategy.
* A limited or poor set of tools available for use by the sales team. You can also probe for this during your sales team and discover how often they use the tools that are available.

If your finding is that there are issues between sales and marketing, don't make the assumption that the fault lies entirely on one side or the other. This is a two-way street, and the source of any issues could lie far back in the history of the organization. Your main task is going to be getting them aligned again with a common goal of getting new customers.

<u>The Channel:</u>

Most companies have channels to market that go beyond their direct sales teams. Whether you are talking about a distributor, a reseller, or a sales-representative firm, a good channel is the best force multiplier that any sales team can have. Most channel partners represent far more than just your offer, giving them both larger customer bases and new-customer traffic that could represent fertile fields for what you are trying to sell. If you are able to get just a small amount of mindshare from all of a channel partner's sales force, you will touch far more customers than your team will ever be able to see on its own.

There are a variety of metrics that you will want to look at for channel partners. Some of these will help you to evaluate specific channel partners, but you should start with a broader view of all of your channel partners combined. For this, you should start with the following:

Percentage of channel partners that grew their business in the previous period
As with your sales force overall, this is a good first indicator of the general health of your channel.

If most of your channel partners are growing, great! Now you have the relatively straightforward problem of just helping those partners to grow more while diving deeper on the ones that are not growing to understand why.

If most of them are not growing, then it is a sign of deeper problems that you have to fix that likely go beyond the channel partners themselves.

Percentage of direct versus indirect accounts
This number was also used in our analysis of the sales team, but we want to look at it in a different light here.

If most of your accounts are led by the channel, you want to be very careful that your salespeople are actually adding value to what the channel salespeople are doing rather than just following them around.

You will get a pretty good sense of this when you interview the top channel partners.

Percentage of joint sales calls made with channel partners
This metric ties directly to the one above it. While joint sales calls are valuable in the right circumstances, the most effective teaming with channel partners happens when everyone is comfortable enough to divide and conquer.

One thing to watch for though: if this percentage is low, you want to confirm that the sales teams are actually communicating with each other. If they are not, then there are going to be problems. As with many other metrics, what you are looking for here is balance.

Number of new customers gained in the last period
This goes to the fundamental question of generating demand versus servicing demand. As discussed with our "leaky-bucket metric" in the sales-team evaluation, a certain number of customers, particularly the small ones, are always going away. This has to be offset by a steady stream of new customers.

Percentage of business from new customers in the previous period
Going beyond measuring the new customers themselves is determining how much impact the revenue from those new customers is having against the overall number. This is likely small when customers are first added, but you want to see a steady increase of impact from this over time.

You can get a good sense of this by looking at this metric over different intervals. For example, looking at the last quarter can show you the immediate impact while looking at the past year will show you if there is a larger impact as new customers ramp up their business with you over time.

Those metrics will give you a good sense of what is going on with your channel overall and will suggest strategic issues that you need to deal with. On a tactical level, you also want to look at the performance of specific channel partners.

When you look at specific channel partners, you will look at a few additional metrics to go along with the metrics listed above. Just be careful that when you look at the metrics now, you keep the context in mind and evaluate them more tactically:

Percentage of their business that your sales represent
This number represents your leverage with that partner and dictates how much mind share you can reasonably expect from the channel

partner and its salespeople. There is a big difference in leverage between being number one on someone's line card and being number thirty.

Percent of growth versus the previous period
Regardless of whether it is up or down, this is a number that will drive a very important part of your conversation with the channel partner. When you meet with the channel partner, you want to get their perspective on the biggest drivers behind its growth or decline. That's the kind of questioning that will lead to a dialogue about how to further improve.

Number of joint sales calls made
As discussed above, there are reasons for both making and not making joint sales calls. Regardless of the number of calls being made, what you want to be sure of is that they are generated from a sound strategy that has been agreed to by both parties. This is another number that can drive meaningful conversation with the channel partner as long as you keep an open-minded approach. Find out the partner's comfort with the current state of circumstances and the reasoning behind this position. With that in mind, you can work out an approach that works for both of you.

Number of new customers in the previous period:
Whatever this number is, it's a big topic for conversation. Are the channel partner's representatives happy with it? If they are, what do they think is working so well to drive it? If not, what do they think is behind it being so low? Real, sustained growth requires new customers.

Once you have the numbers, the most important step is to get out and see the channel partners in person. While you are out in the field on your listening tour with your salespeople, you should see as many of the channel partners as possible. At a minimum, you want to meet with your top ten before you are done.

Channel partners represent the very essence of businesspeople. As the saying goes, if they don't sell, they don't eat. That gives them a real clarity around what your line is or is not doing for them.

When you meet with them, your main objective is simple: listen, listen, listen. There is sure to be a certain amount of griping, but as the great business coach Marshall Goldsmith says, the only proper response to feedback is "Thank you." I will guarantee you that when you have spoken to your top-ten channel partners, common themes about issues in the business are going to emerge. You should treat those themes like gold. They comprise your road map to how you can get even more growth with your channel.

While you have these meetings, keep these big-picture questions in mind. When you finish your tour, they are the ones that you will have to ask yourself about the overall messages that you heard.

* Is your channel creating demand or just servicing it?
* Does the deployment match the opportunities that you want to pursue?
* Is the channel a force multiplier for your sales team?
* Do the channel partners view your team and offer as a key asset or as a burden?
* How easy do the channel partners find your team and company to work with?

What you are looking for:

* Strong collaboration between your salespeople and the channel partners.
* A real culture of growth inside each channel partner.
* A strong desire on the part of the channel partners to continue the relationships.

Red Flags:

- Steady declining sales overall and very little new customer generation. I realize that this probably comes under the "Duh" category. If that is the case with your channel overall, you are already in deep trouble with your number. You are going to have a tough time using the channel as part of any short-term solution. If it's just the case with a few channel partners, you may want to start working on changing out some of the channel partners for new ones, with all of the risk that entails.
- Antagonistic or tense relationships. If things are tense between the company and the channel partner—or, even worse, there has been a breakdown of trust—this needs to go to the very top of your priority list. Peel back the onion until you find the root causes of the issues, be they people or processes, so that you can set a plan to deal with them.
- Complacent salespeople. If you find channel partners who are content to just live with and service the customer base that you already have, then you have to make a tough decision about how they fit into your strategy. There can be value in having people that can do good jobs just holding onto the business that they already have, but if you chose to go in that direction, you need to do it with your eyes wide open.

The Offer

If it were easy to sell a company's offer, then what would they need a sales force for? People would just drive up to the warehouse and demand the product, wouldn't they? While salespeople will often complain about issue A or issue B being the problem with their abilities to sell the offer, it's still the job of the sales team to move the company's offer, regardless of any issues that they have to deal with.

That being said, just as we are going to be brutally honest about how the sales team is performing, we have to be equally frank about what it is that they are given to sell. Please keep in mind, the intent here is not to do a full analysis of a company's offer in the market, but rather to just understand how it is impacting the effectiveness of the sales force.

Percentage of business from new products

This is the primary measure of the heath of new-product development. You can define the time window for "new products" however you want, but it should tie in some way to your average product life.

Looking at products released in the past five years is a good starting point as it takes into account the time that it takes for a new product to catch on and build a base. What denotes a good number here really depends on your overall product strategy, but if most of your sales are coming from very old products, you know that you are getting set up for a competitor to take business away with a new product.

Volume, growth rate, and profitability of each product line along with age and when the next-generation product is coming

Depending on the breadth of your offer, this can end up as a ton of numbers. The trick to working with this data is to look for the outliers.

* Which products are the best and worst for revenue and profitability?
* Which products are getting long in the tooth without something new on the way to refresh them?

Summing that up is going to tell you very quickly how much of a challenge your salespeople are up against in moving the offer.

The overall offer is another topic that you will be gathering information on as you go on your listening tour with the sales, channel-partner, and marketing teams. Some of the questions to keep in mind are:

* How much credibility does the company have with its offer?
* Have past product launches met or missed their promised launch dates and capabilities?
* How well does the offer stack up against the competition?
* Are there any “killer-app” features, or do you have more of a “me-too” product line?
* How much input do the field and channel members feel like they have had toward new-product development and existing-product enhancement?

What you are looking for:

* An offer that has something compelling to differentiate itself from the competition.
* A steady stream of enhancements to the existing products.
* A reasonable flow of new products that are based on real needs from the marketplace.

Red Flags:

* Old and very old product lines that have declining sales and no fit-form-function replacements on the way. These products are going to create a steady deficit that the rest of your offer is going to have to make up. There is always going to be some element of this in an offer, but it has to be at a relatively low proportion to the overall size of the offer.
* Engineering-driven product road maps that don’t have input from the market. I’ve never met an engineer who was not very

proud of what he or she developed, but shelves are filled with great ideas that nobody wanted to pay for.

* A history of missed promises on what products will do or when they will be delivered. Credibility takes years to earn and just seconds to lose. I've always told my sales teams, "Don't sell it until you can drop it on your foot" for a reason. Nothing poisons a customer relationship more than convincing them to work with a new product and then have it be launched very late or not matching the specifications that you promised.

At some point, you will meet with the product-management and engineering teams that are in charge of the offer. You want to be sure that you have a clear understanding of what is driving their decisions around new-product development and new-product enhancement.

Let me tell you the story of the best lesson that I ever got on this front.

> I was running a sales team for a specialized product and was working with a new head of product management and marketing named Susan. She was smart and capable and had turned into a great partner for my sales team and me.
>
> I had just come back from a trip to the field and had the greatest idea for some kind of antigravity module (or something equally great) that we had to add to the product just as soon as possible.
>
> I went to her office and ran through the idea with an impassioned case for why this needed to go to the very top of the priority list for development. The world as we knew it was probably going to end if we did not do it immediately.
>
> After listening patiently to my rant, she looked me right in the eye.

"Be honest with me. Do you need this feature because the market has a real need for it and your sales team is going to be able to get them to pay for it…or do you just want it *because you think it's cool?*"

Wow. What would you do with that?

She did such an amazing job of slapping me back to the reality of business that I married her.

Wrapping It Up

After you conclude your listening tour, it's important to step back, take a bit of time, and think about what you have seen and heard. You have no doubt been doing a bit of this as you have gone along, but there is real value to organizing all of your information, stepping back to look at it with fresh eyes, and thinking about some of the big questions:

What are the main things that are going right in the organization today? What are we doing really well?

Where are the pockets of brilliance? Who are the absolute top talents that you met?

What are the biggest issues that you saw? Which are going to be the top priority to fix?

From this you come to the biggest question of all: What is the strategy going to be? Is it the same one that has been in play? Is it a modification to the existing strategy? Is it a completely new strategy?

Whatever it is, while you are not going to fix everything at once or overnight, you will need to lay out the overall strategy and set priorities with the organization to get everyone on the same page.

If you are intending to do any reorganization at all, get that done first. The team members have been watching you on your listening tour, and the biggest worry that they are going to have is how any changes are going to impact them. For you, it's the big picture. For them, it's personal.

I cannot emphasize enough how critical it is that as soon as you have put this together, you communicate it back out to your team members. They have been watching you conduct this assessment for some time, and now they want to know where you are going to take them. Even if the decision is to change nothing, you need to let them know that and let them know why.

The whole point of this book is how to ensure that our work as sales leaders actually helps our salespeople. Communicating with them fully and frequently is a big part of that.

KEY TAKEAWAYS:

* The primary goal of the assessment is to find the true salespeople, but you also have to find the main issues that are holding your sales team back.
* For a complete view, you have to look at the sales team, the marketing team, the channels that they are working with, and the offer that they have to sell.
* First, get the numbers, and then listen to as many people as possible about what they mean.
* The assessment has to be objective, and you have to force yourself to ignore relationships. Be brutally honest with yourself on every aspect.

Chapter 1-2

What is a True Salesperson?

We're adding a little something to this month's sales contest. As you all know, first prize is a Cadillac Eldorado. Anyone want to see second prize? Second prize is a set of steak knives. Third prize is you're fired.

—*David Mamet, Glengarry Glen Ross*

In David Mamet's movie *Glengarry Glen Ross* (based on his Pulitzer Prize–winning play of the same name), most of the attention goes to Alec Baldwin's seven-minute-long opening diatribe on selling, which I quote from above. It's manic, profane, abusive, and over the top. While it's certainly entertaining to watch, it does not exactly define what most people would call great sales leadership.

Let me tell you a story about a time that I used it with one of my sales teams.

> The company had recently decided to merge two product-sales teams together. One had been growing well, and the other had been declining for several years.

They flew all of the managers from both teams into headquarters, Half of them were sent into one conference room to be fired, and the other half were sent into another conference room to form the new organization.

Luckily, I went to the right conference room.

Luck can be relative though, as we were then told not only about how the organizations were going to be merged but also that to make it work, we were going to have to make significant cuts. They gave us two days to take the list of 150 salespeople in the organization and whittle it down to one hundred.

While that kind of work is sometimes necessary for managers, it is never to be taken lightly, and we struggled to be sure we made the best decisions that we could before we went back to the regions to actually let those fifty people go.

Once we were done with the reduction in force, it was time to bring the combined teams together and get them running. It was spring in San Francisco, where I worked at the time, and I brought my new team in from around the Western US for our first staff meeting, including my brand-new HR and marketing partners.

This was going to be tough. The team that had been underperforming was selling a highly technical product that required a lot of support to make it work. One of the reasons that sales had been poor was that, as with many technical sales organizations, the team was filled with engineers.

Now, I've got nothing against engineers; I happen to be one myself. The issue was that many of the salespeople felt that their primary role was not to close orders but to solve technical problems and "take care of the customer."

> Customer care is pretty important, but in a sales team, at some point, you need to get the customer to buy something.
>
> I knew that I needed to shake the team up, so I queued up a VCR (yes, it was that long ago) and played that seven-minute diatribe from *Glengarry Glen Ross.*
>
> It was about five minutes in when the new marketing partner heard the new HR partner swallow audibly.

Well, to be fair to the HR partner, the profanity in the scene is impressive.

I know that it was probably pretty over the top on my part to play that scene; I had just let several of their buddies go, and now I hit them with "Third prize is you're fired!" That's not exactly going to make people feel more comfortable. I just felt like a message had to be sent. A lot of these folks just were not true salespeople; they were applications engineers. I had to find a way to engage the true salespeople, move out the nonsalespeople, and create a culture of selling in the team.

The central point of this over-the-top speech is a crucial truth about selling: no matter what other elements you want to wrap into your perception of the role of a salesperson, the job comes down to one thing in the end—closing deals. That was the message that I needed them to hear. I had no desire to fire anyone, but the team members needed to get focused on what their job was: closing deals.

That was the first time that I started to think seriously about what made a true salesperson, and after working with hundreds of salespeople since then, I have developed a very methodical approach to my interviewing process and team management to focus on those things.

So, if you boil it down, what are the key elements that define a true salesperson?

An outstanding sales leader named Scott Day taught me about something that he called "bulldog tenacity." Great salespeople see deals that they want to close, and they never let go. They don't wait for something to happen; they make something happen.

Now, that was an insightful rule of thumb from a highly experienced sales leader, but how can you prove it? I've had a few different opportunities to actually look at this objectively. Here is what I was able to find.

There is a company called Revenue Storm that I've had success with in assessing and training my salespeople and managers. Revenue Storm has gone very deep into the question of what makes a successful salesperson, working with literally thousands of salespeople to build their models.

While much of their focus is on their specialized sales training and coaching, one of the most effective things that they sell is an assessment tool for your sales team that they call the Sales Talent Predictor.

This is no quick questionnaire but is a long and deep series of situational questions that ask the candidate how he or she would act in different circumstances. After the salesperson completes the assessment, you get a detailed report that goes far beyond the basic concepts of hunters and farmers. The assessment not only tells you a lot about what type of salesperson you have but also what his or her long-term potential is across several dimensions.

The assessment breaks down the results from the answers into relative strengths across twenty-seven sales competencies, such as managing objections and negotiating, as well as thirty-four attributes of the salesperson, such as stress tolerance or initiative.

Obviously, this is a very complex breakdown of a salesperson, and it takes a combination of Revenue Storm's training and consulting to help a manager properly interpret and act on the data in the coaching and development of salespeople.

With one team that I ran, we decided to peel back the onion a little bit further. We wanted to know if there were any particular attributes that most strongly correlated with success. We had a data set of both the sales results and the Sales Talent Predictor assessments for the sixty salespeople who were working with me at that time. We put that data through a huge amount of analysis to see if we could find which elements or combination of elements most strongly correlated with success.

This is the first instance in which Scott Day's rule of thumb was proven. There was a clearly defined correlation between sales performance and the "initiative" attribute from the assessment. Salespeople with the highest assessed levels of initiative tended to have the highest sales performances.

In a similar analysis at another company, we did an objective evaluation of how proactively the person was using the CRM tool that we had in place versus the sales results that he or she was getting.

Certain elements of how salespeople use CRM clearly indicate how much initiative they are taking, and this was used to build an "initiative index" from the historical CRM data. Twenty-one metrics were used to build the index, but some of the key elements brought into this were:

* Number of sales calls made.
* Percentage of sales calls planned in advance.
* Frequency of updates on deals.
* Use of the next steps function of the CRM on deals.

When these were plotted against sales performance, the correlation was striking as people coalesced into three distinct groups:

* Group A was barely using the CRM tool proactively and had the worst sales results.
* Group B was using the CRM tool with some degree of proactivity and getting decent results.

* Group C was being very proactive with the CRM tool and getting outstanding results.

Even with outliers, these groups were very strongly correlated. We did not have any cases of strong users getting poor results or weak users getting good results.

Certainly, these are small statistical universes, but they do clearly illustrate the point about how important initiative is in a salesperson. In my opinion, it is the single most predictive attribute for a salesperson's success.

Going back to the work done by Revenue Storm, the makeup of a true salesperson is more than just initiative. The main thing to keep in mind about the company's work is that it breaks down the makeup of the salesperson into two parts: the attributes of who he or she is and the person's competency with the skills that he or she has been taught.

This proposition goes back to the age-old "nature versus nurture" debate that we discussed earlier in the book. While I am sure that many people will argue the point, my experience has shown me that you have to have the attributes of a true salesperson in the first place if training is going to have any real value. You can figure out the attributes that mean the most to you, but this is the list that I have worked out over the years.

True salespeople take the initiative.
I've probably already beaten this one to death, but you can't underestimate the importance of this personality characteristic.

True salespeople listen.
It's ironic that the classic expression in sales has always been "two ears, one mouth" while the stereotype of the salesperson is of the glib fast-talker. A true salesperson is an active listener and a skilled questioner who gets a deep understanding of what a customer's needs are before he or she ever pitches anything.

True salespeople follow up.
This is something so basic but so rarely done. Too many salespeople are great in the room, promise to get things done, and then promptly let the whirlwind take over and never meet those promises. Customers remember the salespeople that follow through on their commitments—and they remember the ones that don't even more.

True salespeople are accountable.
The only place a true salesperson looks for fault is in the mirror. This does not mean that salespeople have to beat themselves up all the time, but when things go wrong, they don't blame it on outside circumstances. True salespeople focus on what they could have done to better deal with the outside circumstances that arose and learn from them for the next time.

True salespeople hate to lose deals or miss their numbers.
Nothing makes me more concerned than a salesperson who is nonchalant when a deal is lost or when he or she misses quota. True salespeople take their responsibilities seriously and understand that other jobs in the organization depend on them bringing in the revenue.

True salespeople are natural relationship builders.
To take liberty with the old real-estate maxim, there are three things that determine who is going to win an order; relationship, relationship, and relationship. If a deal revolves around price, then winning it does not involve salesmanship.

True salespeople are gifted storytellers.
They use stories to illustrate their points, and they tell them clearly, concisely, and compellingly.

Each of these statements maps directly back to specific attributes in the Revenue Storm model, and it is my contention that if you don't have these specific elements in the makeup of your salespeople, then you are wasting your time trying to train them on skills. The bottom line is that they simply are not wired as salespeople.

So how do you get there?

Step one is to be brutally honest with yourself about the people whom you have on the team now. If employees are not true salespeople, then you have to face the fact that no matter how nice they are, how long that they have been with your company, or how many training programs you send them to, they are never going to genuinely succeed in sales.

When you identify the individuals who are not true salespeople and you have some meaningful conversations with them, you are going to find some common elements. Here is one of the most fundamental tests: What are they thinking when they get out of bed in the morning on the days when they make sales calls?

While the true salespeople are the most excited to get at the day when they know that they are going to make sales calls, the pretenders tend to hate getting out of bed on those days. In their hearts, they have to psych themselves up for it.

This does not mean that they are not useful people, but it does mean that they are not the salespeople that you need—because they are not really salespeople in the first place. They are in the wrong jobs. The best thing that you can do for them is to help them come to that realization and try to find the careers that actually fit them and where they will have the best chances to excel.

These can be some of the hardest conversations to have, but I can tell you that over the years, I have had people come to me after they have moved on and actually thank me for helping to get them out of sales and into something where they could succeed.

Step two is to be equally objective when you are evaluating new people for your team. Pick an evaluation system like Revenue Storm's or a structured interview, and use it consistently for every candidate, no matter how much you "like" the person after the interview process.

There are plenty of firms out there offering to train and evaluate teams. There are also all kinds of selling methodologies to teach your teams—from SPIN selling to Challenger to Miller Heiman to Revenue Storm. What you pick is going to depend on the type of selling that your products and business model require.

In the end, the exact program does not matter as much as how serious you are about using it. I can't tell you how many times I have seen companies spend huge amounts of money and time training their salespeople only to fail to ensure that the methodology was used in the business going forward.

Just keep one thing in mind as you start to invest in any kind of sales training. Effective sales training is a process, not an event. It needs to be reinforced with consistent coaching from the sales managers immediately following the training and in all of their coaching sessions going forward. Completing the training is not the end—it's the beginning.

KEY TAKEAWAYS:

* The single most predictive characteristic for identifying a true salesperson is initiative.
* True salespeople take initiative, listen, follow up, are accountable, hate losing, hate missing their numbers, and are natural relationship builders and gifted storytellers.
* Unless you are serious about setting this kind of a capability bar with your sales team, you will never get to the top levels of performance for your team.

Chapter 1-3

An Interview That Finds the True Salespeople

Interviewing a new person for a role is something that most managers are well acquainted with, but it's a slightly different task when you are evaluating people who are already in their positions. That is what we have to do to complete the kind of assessment that we will be talking about in this chapter.

My favorite example of this kind of interview has always been the scene with the "Bobs" in Mike Judge's movie *Office Space*.

> In the scene, a young man named Peter Gibbons is interviewing with two consultants—both named Bob.
>
> Peter is not exactly a determined employee, but as the scene goes on, he keeps blowing the two interviewers away because unlike everyone else that they have ever interviewed, he is being completely honest.
>
> Almost insanely honest—and they love it.
>
> Peter tells them how messed up management is and how he barely puts in any effort as a result. He finishes up the interview with a candid comment that would normally get anyone fired on the spot.

"The thing is, Bob, it's not that I'm lazy. *It's that I just don't care*"

Naturally, he gets a promotion.

Whether or not the issue there was with the employee or management, the consultants are getting something that you rarely get in an interview—complete honesty. Most interviews are a bit of a dance with each party trying to position itself with the other. It takes skillful questioning to get a high degree of candor, particularly if you are new to a team and have no real background to give context to your interview.

When you take over a new team, it's critical to understand the existing population of salespeople. Part of this is understanding whether they are true salespeople or not, but you are also trying to figure out just what types of salespeople they are so that you can work out how to best deploy them.

What are the right questions to actually zero in on the characteristics that we discussed for true salespeople? In this chapter, you will find the ones that I have found to really illuminate those characteristics. I've used the interview described below hundreds of times, and it has evolved to help me determine both who the true salespeople are as well as their types and skill levels.

For the purposes of our listening tour, the basic interview discussed earlier will work adequately. If you feel that you need to go deeper and get an in-depth assessment of a team, then this is a better tool for it. Just keep in mind that this is an in-depth interview. Done properly, it will take sixty to ninety minutes to conduct.

If you are the leader of a large sales organization, you will probably not have the time to do many of these, but it can be informative to do a representative sample in different regions. Regional managers should consider doing this interview with all of the people on their teams, even if it is done over a long period of time.

Keep in mind, while the context of this chapter is the evaluation of existing teams, this interview should also be used when evaluating any new hires as well.

How you set up the meeting is critical. Any interview is going to make the subject nervous. You have to respect the person's intelligence and put the whole thing in perspective.

One way to do this is to explain the purpose of the interview to the salespeople in terms of a sports coach. In the United States, we tend to use American football. Around the rest of the world, we typically use soccer.

> "Thanks for coming in today. I can only imagine that you might be a bit nervous about this meeting, so let me try to help you keep it in perspective.
>
> "Think of me as the coach of an American football team. I've just taken over, but before I can decide on what kind of a game plan I am going to put together for the season, I need to understand what type of players I have on my team.
>
> "If I've got a world-class running back and an overpowering offensive line, I might base everything around the ground game. If I've got a Hall of Fame receiver and quarterback, I'd be nuts not to base my plans on throwing the ball.
>
> "That's all I'm trying to do today—figure out what types of players I have on my team.
>
> "What I really want to do here is have a conversation with you about selling and have you tell me some stories about deals and customers. Are you comfortable with that?"

From there, you can take it in any direction and use the questions that work best for you, but there are some critical guidelines that you should keep in mind regardless of the specific questions.

* You should be consistent in the questions that you ask from person to person. This lets you evaluate them against each other objectively.
* Take good notes. Really good notes. If you are interviewing a bunch of people, it will be hard to keep your memory straight later. Taking notes also serves to make you more of an active listener.
* If you can manage it, having another person in the room with you can help, but this is a double-edged sword as it can make some interviewees even more nervous.
* The best salespeople are great storytellers. All of your questions should be set up to get them to tell stories, but you also need to be ready to shut them down if they ramble on or start to go off on tangents. If it happens too much, it's a good indicator of how well the salesperson can read the person to whom they are talking and detect when he or she has gone on too long.

My normal interview has a few more questions that draw out someone's background and serve as icebreakers, and you should use whichever ones fit your style the best. This is really more about getting them talking comfortably.

"What can you tell me about your background?"

"Where did you grow up?"

"Where did you go to school?"

Here are the more substantive questions that have worked best and how they should be interpreted.

"Tell me the story of how you came to take your first job in sales."

This is a pretty nonthreatening story to try and get someone to tell you. By design, it will get them into "storytelling" mode for some of the tougher stories later on.

What you are looking for:

* How passionately the person tells the story and what the person tells you about how he or she came to be in sales should tell you a lot about his or her motivation as a salesperson and how much this person considers it to be their profession.

Red Flags:

* In a perfect world, you only want people on your team who really, really want to be there. If you get any ambivalence from them about the pride that they take in their roles, it's worth peeling that onion back a bit with some probing questions. This does not have to be fancy; you can go right to the point with something like "From your story, I'm not picking up a lot of passion about the sales profession. Am I misreading that?"

"We know your official job description, but in your own words, what do you do?"

The first time I heard this question from a channel partner named Dan Keenan, I thought it was a bit basic, but once I started asking it, its power was clear. When someone tells you the job description on the spot, you are getting the person's top-of-mind thoughts on what the most important elements of the job are.

What you are looking for:

* A clear and concise description of what the person does.

Red Flags:

* If the tasks of making sales calls and closing deals do not have starring roles, you have to question if the person really understands the priorities of the position.
* If the salesperson rambles all over the place, that can indicate that he or she is not good at answering questions clearly. Ask yourself how that might play out with a customer.
* If the salesperson editorializes about the position, making excuses for performance instead of offering solutions to issues in the business that may come up, that can indicate attitude issues or broader morale problems in the organization.

"I'd like you to think about your list of accounts, and in your mind, pick out your favorite one or one that you find particularly interesting. I am going to ask you some questions about it. What account comes to mind?

"Can you tell me briefly what they do?"

"What do they use our products for today?"

"In one or two sentences, can you tell me what your overall strategy is for the account?"

"Can you tell me the three key tactics that you must execute to make that strategy happen this year?

This question (and the questions that follow it next) are the more complicated ones to ask as you have to keep them sectioned off and ask them in sequence to keep people from rambling all over the place. In this case, you ask it as a series of five questions. The first four have very short answers, and the fifth is longer.

It can be tough to facilitate the question because even when you stick to this exact wording, people will often launch into long stories that do not get to the point of what you are looking for. Don't be afraid to cut people off if they start to run off on a tangent. You can do it very politely with a quick comment: "Can you hold that thought for a moment? I've got some specific things that I want to ask you about this account."

What you are looking for:

* The first thing that you are looking for is emotional engagement. Does the salesperson care about the account and what he or she is doing with it? Is this something that is being pursued with vigor, or is the person just marking time? You can see this in everything from body language to how much animation is brought to the story that he or she is telling.
* You want to see if the person has a clear, concise, and compelling plan for what he or she wants to do with the account. You are also looking to see if people understand the difference between strategy and tactics and how to think about that with their accounts.
* A strategy is an overall plan, while the tactics are the things that you do to execute that plan.
* A good example of an account strategy and tactic might be as follows:

  "My strategy for this account is to make myself valuable to the customer as a business partner by bringing opportunities for new customers to him."

  "Tactically, I am going to conduct monthly reviews of our major product bids and find at least one that I can bring in this customer to be a subcontractor on."

Red Flags:

* Not being able to decide on an account.
* Lack of energy or animation in talking about the account and what he or she is doing with it.
* Confusing goals and objectives of the account with strategy and tactics.
* Presenting a strategy and tactics that do not really make sense to drive growth of a customer.

Depending on how good an answer you get and how much time you think that you have, you may want to ask the salesperson about more than one account.

"I'd like you to think about your current pipeline of deals, and in your mind, pick out your favorite one or one that you find particularly interesting. I am going to ask you some questions about it. Which deal would you like to talk about?"

"What is the deal for? What are we selling?"

"What is the central value proposition that you are making to the customer? Why would they want to buy it from us?"

"What is your next actionable step on the deal?"

As with the previous question, you have to be careful not to let the answer run all over the place and to ask the question in sequence.

What you really want to see are some signs of emotional engagement. If I have a salesperson getting more and more excited as he or she talks about the pursuit of the deal, I tend to let the person run with it a bit. That kind of emotion is hard to fake and is the mark of a true competitor.

What you are looking for:

- This answer is going to tell you a lot about how the salesperson thinks about the deals. The most important thing that you are looking for is a salesperson with an overall plan for attacking the deal, as opposed to someone who is just reacting to what happens as time goes on. The best salespeople are able to break up any deal into expected milestones, and they know where they stand in that process and how they are going to navigate their way through it.
- The last question in the next step is the most critical one. It is going to tell you quite a bit about the initiative and commercial intensity of the salesperson. The best salespeople will have next steps that are very clear, time based, and designed to actually move the deal forward. The answers will come right off the tips of their tongues because they're extremely important to them.

Red Flags

- Not being able to have a specific deal come to mind. Someone might have a hard time deciding between a few particularly interesting deals, but a true salesperson always has a particular deal that is top of mind at the moment.
- Not showing excitement about the deal as the person describes it. The pursuit of a deal is the most exciting thing to a salesperson, and you should see it.
- If someone has to think about the next step too long. If it's not on the tip of the tongue, then the person has not already thought it out, and he or she certainly is not in the process of executing it. True salespeople think about deals a few steps ahead, like chess masters, and will also have the next few steps in their minds as well.

* Any passive element to the next step, such as "waiting for the customer to get back to me," is the most serious of red flags. Pay attention to both the words and the attitude here. If the salesperson is not taking the initiative to move the deal forward, then this employee is probably not a true salesperson.

"You've been in sales for a long time, and I am sure that you have closed plenty of deals. I'd like you to think back over your career and tell me the story of the deal that you are proudest of. It can be any size or type of deal; it just has to be one that you really love what you did to win it. Can you tell me the story of that deal?"

"In any deal, there always seems to be a moment before the customer actually tells you that you have the order, when you just know that you have won. Can you tell me about that moment on this deal?"

This is what I think of as my "money question." The answer to it tends to tell the most about the salesperson and how he or she thinks about a deal. It's also a very fair question since you are not cherry-picking a particular deal; you are allowing the person to pick from any deal that he or she wants. The best salespeople are going to tend to have more than one come to mind, and you often have to tell them to just pick one, but if the salesperson is on a roll and time allows for it, I will let them tell me about two.

What you are looking for:

* If ever you want to see animation in someone telling the story, this is the time. People should show their pride in these deals and particularly in what they did to win them. If they start to go on and on, I tend to let them ramble for a bit as long as the stories have some structure. If they are going all over the place, you can ask some clarifying questions to get them back on track:

"So just what were you selling?"

"What did the customer need?"

"How did you come to be involved in the deal in the first place?"

Be cautious if you have to do too much of this. The best salespeople are natural storytellers. They should be able to tell clear, concise, and compelling stories about the deals.

* What you are really looking for is the part of the story that tells what the salesperson did to create the demand or get it to closure. Asking about the closing moment is one way to get at it, but it can also come out in other ways. What you want to see is that the person did something concrete in the approach that changed the trajectory of the deal. If he or she was just passively waiting for something to happen, you have to question why the person would pick that deal to talk about and what it tells you about the employee as a salesperson.
* One subtler element of the answer is going to center around how someone picked this deal as one to be proud of. Is the person proud of the deal because of what was done to close it or just because of the size of it? Closing a million-dollar deal because you were the low bid is not real selling, but closing it with a higher price because you convinced the customer that you had the best overall value sure is.

Red Flags:

* If you get the deer-in-the-headlights look and the person can't think of a deal. If it's just a case of not being able to decide between multiple deals, that is OK, but any experienced salesperson

should have a whole list of wins that he or she is proud of and eager to tell you a story about.

* When someone tells the story, if you can't tell what the person actually did to win the deal. The salesperson should know precisely what he or she actively did and show some pride in telling you about it. If it looks like this person was just along for the ride and administering a transaction, then you need to be very concerned. If you are not sure, you can ask some probing questions to uncover actions. You can also consider letting the salesperson tell you about a second deal to see if that gives you a better sense of their approach.

"In our careers, we work with a lot of different salespeople, both good and bad. The best ones are often the ones we end up emulating ourselves as time goes on. When you think about all of the salespeople you have worked with, can you tell me who was the best salesperson that you ever saw?"

"Why?"

"How do you think that are you different as a salesperson from that person? I don't mean better or worse, just different."

The particular person chosen for the answer here is not the real answer to the question. What we are looking for is how the interviewee thinks about what makes a great salesperson. The employee describes that person, talking about the qualities that he or she sees as being the most important ones for the profession.

What you are looking for:

* In the hundreds of times that I have asked this question, by far the most common answer is an early manager who really coached the salesperson and helped them become who he or she is. You get some real emotion coming out when the salesperson talks about

his or her influence and the impact that the person had. This is often worth probing to try to get the salesperson to tell a story about that influence that can serve as an example.

* The last part of the question can be a bit tricky as, no matter how well you phrase it, it tends to get received as how the interviewee is better or worse than that person. Even if the person named is someone that your employee has completely tried to emulate, there should still be differences that the salesperson can be honest enough about to discuss.

Red Flags

* If the salesperson really can't think of anyone.
* If he or she can't come up with elements in describing that person that reflect on real sales skills and can only give general platitudes like "he was a great guy."

"Over the course of our careers, we've all worked on a lot of deals and projects. Sometimes they go very well, and sometimes they go very badly. Sometimes when they go bad, it is because of something that the universe did to us, and sometimes it's because we made a mistake. Can you tell me about the biggest professional mistake that you ever made on a deal and, most importantly, what you learned from it?"

The classic "tricky" interview question has always been "What is your greatest weakness?" We have all heard countless answers to this—mostly of the self-serving "I work too hard" or "I'm too much of a perfectionist" types. This question tries to get around that by making it about telling a specific story.

Most of these questions, if answered thoughtfully, will come with a pause before the salesperson starts to give the answer. This question tends to have the longest pause and also has the highest rate of not being answered at all. Believe it or not, I have actually gotten the "I've never made a mistake" answer—and more than once!

The idea here is not to embarrass the salesperson by forcing him or her to tell a negative story, but it is to see if the salesperson can objectively look at the sales process and, in the same way that he or she told us about a win, tell us about a loss.

What you are looking for:

* An understanding of not just that the salesperson made a mistake but why it was a mistake.
* A clear ownership of the mistake. The best answers that you get to this are almost proud of the mistake, not in terms of having made the mistake but in terms of what the salesperson was able to take away from it and the deals that have been won since then by not making that same mistake again.

Red Flags:

* Not being able to come up with a mistake. I've given people a lot of time to answer this; it's not an expected question. However, if they really can't think of an example, it should raise big questions in your mind.
* Making the story really be about someone else's mistake that the salesperson was just involved in. This is a very common response, and while it's understandable that someone does not want to say anything negative about him or herself, I have real concerns about someone who points to another person as an excuse. The salesperson has to "own" mistakes.

"If you could change any one thing at the company—but only one thing—what would you want to change?"

I often call this the "magic-wand question." In one team evaluation, I actually carried a little magic wand around in my briefcase to help break things up a bit. This is a wind-down question as you close out the interview, but it's still an important one as it can show how critically the salesperson is thinking about the current organization.

As a new leader, the answers to this question can be invaluable as you will inevitably find common threads across the organization that will help you to prioritize the biggest issues in the team.

When you get an answer, it's important to probe a bit:

> "Why is this issue important to you?"
>
> "How is it impacting your day-to-day life?"
>
> "What have you tried to do to fix it in the past? What happened?"
>
> What you are looking for:

* Ideas that tie to real issues that you know you have in the business. This gives you confirmation of the issue and some case-study information to give more depth to your understanding of what is happening.
* Issues that have not yet hit your radar at all. If you get one of these, be sure to probe more deeply to ensure that you fully understand the issue and are not making any assumptions.

> Red Flags:

* Giving a trivial or flip response. If the salesperson is truly invested in the organization, he or she will have a list of things that need to be done better, and the biggest problem for the salesperson is deciding on which is number one. My favorite answers to this question come when salespeople beg me to let them name a second item.

"What questions do you have for me?"

I always like to close out with this to make the dialogue reciprocal and get a higher degree of engagement. When you do this, it's important that you give thoughtful answers and write down any commitments that you make in response to the questions raised.

If you are doing this as a high-level leader in the course of this interview, you have been building a relationship with one of your front-line resources to whom you may not speak directly again for some time. If you react to the questions that are important to them and show that you valued their importance, then you are building real bonds that will last into the future.

One of the most common questions that you will be asked, particularly from a true salesperson, is "How did I do in this interview?" It's important to note that this is not a performance review and that you don't want to make a person feel like this is a one-dimensional evaluation. This should be just one data point out of many to help you to get a better sense of who he or she is as a salesperson.

Remember how you set the interview up, and frame your answer in those terms. Remind them that your intent is to figure out the types of players you have on your team as you build up your overall game plan.

If someone asks this question, you are given an avenue for a productive dialogue. You can give your impression of what type of salesperson he or she is and then get the person's thoughts on why he or she does or does not agree with that. Even more meaningfully, you can have a dialogue about how well the person feels that their current assignment aligns with his or her type.

You should close the interview by telling the interviewee that you really enjoyed the conversation and feel like you have a much better understanding of who he or she is.

What you are looking for:

* Thoughtful questions about what is behind the strategies and policies that you have been driving if you are the existing leader.
* Thoughtful questions about what you think about the prior strategies and policies if you are just coming in as a new leader.
* Thoughtful suggestions about where the business could and should be going.
* Questions about what is going on in the business.
* Questions about what you see your competition doing.

Red Flags:

* Not having any questions ready at all. If a salesperson walks into this meeting with a superior or senior leader and does not plan on some questions, you have to ask yourself how prepared he or she is when walking into a customer meeting.

KEY TAKEAWAYS:

* It takes skillful questioning to get past the natural "dance" that is going to go on in this kind of an interview.
* The most important questions are the ones that get the salesperson to tell you stories about accounts, deals, salespeople, and mistakes.
* With each story, you will get more and more insight into how the salesperson thinks about selling.
* For each type of story, there are elements that will show you if they are true salespeople, and there are red flags that will tell you that they are not.

Chapter 1-4

Coaching Like You Mean It

I'm a very firm believer that the primary role of any sales manager is to act as a coach for the team. Whether they think about it explicitly in those terms or not, many of the best sales managers do this every day, and the result of it can be seen in both the productivity and the morale of their teams.

You can also see pretty clearly when they don't.

> Joe was a salesman whom I worked with for many years, and he was good—almost crazy good. Joe has that special gift that lets him network all through a company, building supporters along the way until he hits the big decision makers in the C suite.
>
> Customers loved working with Joe because he was so interested in them and their problems. He was always asking questions and listening. As a salesperson, he was as successful as one could get, working strategic accounts and making sure that the folks in our factories had jobs.
>
> As one would expect, after a certain amount of time, Joe was moved into a sales-leadership role. To say that what happened next was a train wreck would be to do a disservice to train wrecks.

The team that he was asked to lead, filled with top salespeople like Joe, was ready to mutiny within a few short months, calling other leaders in the organization and begging for help.

Why? When Joe would go on sales calls with his team, he would take the meeting over. His approach with his team seemed to be "I'm a great salesperson. Watch me at work, and do what I do, and you will become great as well."

To the salespeople on his team, this was beyond insulting, and even the customers found it presumptuous as they watched the salespeople with whom they had worked for some time be shunted aside in the sales calls.

The irony was that the very thing that made Joe great as a salesperson—his skill in determining his customers' true needs—was something that he failed to take advantage of when he moved into a leadership role.

He didn't listen and learn the needs of his salespeople and their strategies for customers prior to going on the joint calls with them.

His boss tried to help him out, but the damage was done with the team, and Joe returned to a strategic sales position, this time working for me. We went on a long journey together to help both of us understand what had happened and learn from it.

To his immense credit, Joe never stuck his head in the sand. Once we got to the point at which he realized what had really happened, Joe genuinely embraced his mistake and what he learned from it.

Joe became a valuable partner to me in running our team, and I came to lean on his counsel frequently as he developed into a capable and effective sales leader.

What really happened here? In making his first move to a leadership role, Joe made the mistake of conflating management and leadership—and the leaders around him made the mistake of assuming that even though he was a first-time manager, he'd had enough of the right kind of coaching to know the difference.

Did Joe intend to act in a way that would disrespect and alienate his sales team? Absolutely not! I think that if I could go back in time to ask him in the moment, he would say that he was doing his best to help his salespeople. There is no doubt at all that Joe's heart was in the right place.

Joe, like most managers, wanted to coach his team and genuinely thought that he was doing so by showing them his "example." It was more efficient that way. Talking things through ahead of time and debriefing afterward takes time.

That gets us to the core of this problem: time. Real coaching takes time, and time is a commodity in short supply in any sales organization. While the daily whirlwind of things is happening, salespeople and sales managers are getting hammered from above about whatever their short-term result is, and long-term coaching tends to fall to the wayside.

In that situation, the salespeople don't see the good intentions of the sales manager; they just see the hammer. It takes a conscious effort for a sales manager to slow things down and provide coaching instead of just direction.

I'll never forget working with a sales manager named Rich when I was just starting out. Even though I did not work for him, Rich was always willing to offer coaching to me when I needed it (which was often). What really made an impact on me was the way that Rich would signal that I had his complete attention when he coached me.

When I would come into his office to ask for help, he would listen to my initial question and then take the papers in front of him (we used paper back then), fold them up, and carefully put them to the side of his desk. It was a subtle little trick, but it left no doubt in my mind that he was focused on my situation in that moment.

Slowing down and making time is just the first step. The next step is even harder: delivering real coaching. In any job—sales, marketing, engineering, or manufacturing—the front-line person is often already an expert. What this person normally needs from a boss is not direction, it's really just help to see things from a different vantage point. A great coach does not tell people what to do; a great coach helps them tell themselves what to do.

From this perspective, probably the most famous coach of all time lived over 2,400 years ago in Ancient Greece. His name was Socrates and the method that he is famous for has stood the test of thousands of years of education. The method is based on asking questions to stimulate thinking rather than simply lecturing.

Just like a bad coach, a weak teacher can just hold forth at the front of the room vomiting answers out to students. Is that really going to drive learning? What the best teachers want is for the students to think about the material and offer up their insights. They know that the students will retain the information that they gain in that way as true knowledge.

The right way to coach a salesperson is to help him or her to solve problems independently, through the use of insightful questions.

Done properly, this allows salespeople to sort through all of the noise around their problems and focus on the right things. The sales world is filled with distractions, and often the best thing that a manager can give them is the right kind of sounding board to figure out where to best apply their efforts.

The answer to the problem is almost always in the salesperson's head; the sales manager just has to draw it out.

That can be tough to do, particularly when you are rushed. Think about a typical situation where a salesperson brings a problem to a manager. With his or her experience, the sales manager probably already knows a viable solution to the problem and can direct the salesperson to go do A, B, and C in response to the situation. The sales manager is busy, and the time that was set aside to talk to the salesperson is quickly running out.

To do this right, the sales manager has to resist the temptation to just give an answer and be patient while walking the salesperson through the thinking that will get him or her to the solution.

In the long run, this actually means *less* work for the sales manager, because the manager is teaching the salesperson how to think through the situation. The trick for the sales manager is to be ready with a pattern of questions to draw out the salesperson in any situation.

The best way that I have found to do this is a variation on the "five-whys" technique that was developed at Toyota to find the root cause of problems in the manufacturing process. The idea is that when you are faced with a problem, you just keep digging down multiple layers by asking more "Why?" questions.

The engine died.

Why?

There was no oil.

Why?

It leaked out.

Why?

The oil-drain plug was loose.

Why?

It was not torqued down properly.

Why?

We did not have a torque wrench and a specification for torquing it properly during manufacturing.

The same idea can apply to sales situations. It also gets even more powerful when augmenting *why* with *what, who,* and *how* questions.

So that's where the deal stands right now.

What do you think it will take to move it forward to the next step?

Well, it's got to get overall production approval.

Who do you think the key person is for that?

It's either Bill or Susan.

How do you think that you can find out for sure?

I'm pretty sure that John will know for sure. I can call him after this meeting and find out.

What could motivate Bill to sign it?

I don't know.

What is Bill's primary measurement in his job?

Keeping the line running.

What about the solution that you are proposing could impact that?

There is no set number of how many whys, whats, whos, and hows to use. You just have to be sure that all of them are open-ended questions that get the salesperson to think more deeply about the situation—one that they know far more intimately than you do.

Any real coaching is going to center around a question-based dialogue with the salesperson.

While this basic questioning methodology is going to be consistent through all of the coaching that you do, some of the specifics of how you manage the questioning will depend on the type of environment that you are in.

For a start, let's discuss three fundamental environments and how to specifically adapt the methodology: structured coaching, joint sales calls, and ad-hoc coaching.

<u>Structured Coaching</u>

There have been numerous studies on the benefits of structured coaching and how much salespeople appreciate it, particularly from the Corporate Executive Board. I've found their work in this area to be particularly insightful and it has really proven itself out to me as I applied it in the real world.

Let's start by defining it. Structured coaching is comprised of regular, scheduled, one-on-one coaching sessions between a manager and a salesperson. The agenda is preset so that the salesperson knows in advance what is going to be discussed and what to be prepared for.

Here are some basic rules to follow for successful structured-coaching sessions:

- The sessions have to be focused on coaching, not inspection or micromanagement.

* The sessions should be at regular intervals with each salesperson and scheduled out for the year.
* The frequency can vary depending on the number of reports and their maturity as salespeople, but it should never be spread out more than monthly. For experienced salespeople, I've found that every two weeks is a good interval.
* The sales manager needs to do his or her best not to move these meetings around. The real world will certainly force some reschedules, but the manager needs to minimize them to show the salesperson that this time, and thus he or she, is a priority.
* The flow of the meeting needs to be consistent from session to session as it creates a comfortable environment for the salesperson. A salesperson can walk into the meeting knowing that he or she has prepared properly.
* The manager absolutely needs to set time aside prior to the meeting to ensure preparation. If the salesperson has put time and effort into putting data into the CRM tool or sending e-mails to the manager, then the manager needs to be sure to have read it all prior to the meeting. When the sales manager does that, this shows the salesperson that he or she values the input. It also reinforces the need to use the CRM tool and keep it current. Investing time in preparation also allows for more discussion time in the meeting instead of having it feel like a reporting session for the salesperson.
* Even the most dedicated managers can let regular coaching fall to the wayside, particularly with their top performers. The sales managers have to be sure to watch out for this. One simple trick is for sales managers to simply keep logs of how many coaching sessions (of all types) they are doing with their teams. This will often uncover unconscious bias in the use of the sales managers' time. Having the right balance is important.

The sales manager should work out a flow for these meetings that works best for how they are running their sales teams. The exact content will also depend on just which functions they have put into their CRM tools and are expecting their salespeople to be utilizing, such as sales-call planning.

One example of the kind of structured-coaching sessions that I am talking about here would be this:

Sales-Call Questions

Prior to the meeting, the manager should take a look at the most recent sales call plans and ask:

> Are the sales call plans clear, concise, and compelling?
>
> Did every call have follow-up actions, and were they managed in the CRM?

Doing this prework both prepares the manager for areas on which to coach the salesperson and also reinforces to the salesperson that the manager considers the meeting important.

When the manager asks about individual sales call results, there are some specific questions to ask to draw out how the person was thinking about the call:

> What would you like to have done differently in the sales call? Why?
>
> What is your next step with that customer? What will that do for you?

When the manager talks about the overall portfolio of sales calls, there are specific, probing questions that can uncover how the salesperson is thinking about them:

> Did you hit your goal for planning sales calls and making sales calls? If not, what kept you from meeting the goal? What help do you need to remove that barrier in the future?

Which calls were on new customers? How did those calls come about?

Pipeline Questions

Prior to the meeting, the manager should take a look at the current pipeline for the salesperson and ask themselves:

Is all of the opportunity data current in the CRM? (Particular attention should be paid to close date, sales stage, next step, next-step date, and forecast category)

Do all of the deals have meaningful and actionable next steps?

When talking about the overall pipeline with the salesperson, the manager should try to drive focus with these probing questions:

What are the top three deals that you are currently working to close for this period?

What are the most important things that you need to get done to close those deals this period?

What could prevent those deals from closing? What can you do to mitigate that risk?

What have you done this week to advance those deals?

To manage the structure of these coaching sessions, it's best to have some preconfigured reports or scorecards for each salesperson that gives the manager a snapshot of where the salesperson stands. The manager should be able to easily pull and review these scorecards prior to the start of the coaching session.

One example of this is an account-activity scorecard. All too often, the state of a salesperson's account portfolio is only viewed in terms of the overall sales versus prior year or quota. The problem with that view is that it does not incorporate a measure of the activities that are leading indicators of future growth. The longer that your sales cycle is, the more important it is to keep an eye on these leading indicators.

The account-activity scorecard below is designed to provide that view at a glance and focuses on both the current state as well as leading indicators that show how the sales result is being built for the future. As long as you have your account planning and sales calls built into your CRM, you can build a report like this fairly easily.

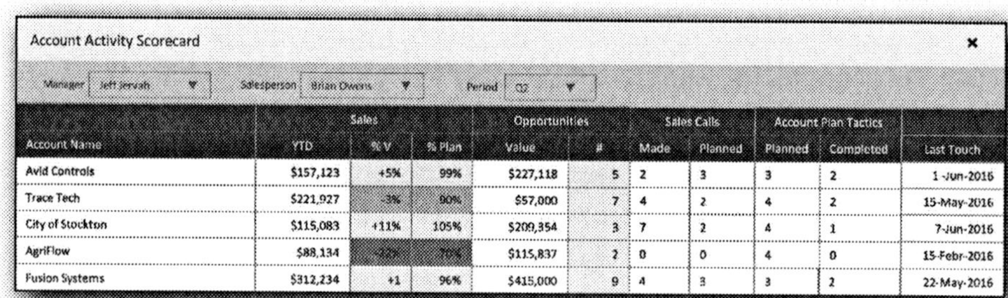

Account Activity Scorecard

Manager: Jeff Jervah | Salesperson: Brian Owens | Period: Q2

	Sales			Opportunities		Sales Calls		Account Plan Tactics		
Account Name	YTD	% V	% Plan	Value	#	Made	Planned	Planned	Completed	Last Touch
Avid Controls	$157,123	+5%	99%	$227,118	5	2	3	3	2	1-Jun-2016
Trace Tech	$221,927	-3%	90%	$57,000	7	4	2	4	2	15-May-2016
City of Stockton	$115,083	+11%	105%	$209,354	3	7	2	4	1	7-Jun-2016
AgriFlow	$88,134	-22%	70%	$115,837	2	0	0	4	0	15-Febr-2016
Fusion Systems	$312,234	+1	96%	$415,000	9	4	3	3	2	22-May-2016

(Figure 1.4.1)

Sales

This is the most basic view of sales performance. How much has the salesperson sold to the account, how does it compare to the previous period, and how does it compare to plan? A good tool allows these results to automatically color code so that marginal or poor performance jumps off the page. Not every account is going to grow in every period, but if the view of a salesperson's portfolio has too much yellow or red in it, the sales manager knows to dive in there.

Opportunities

For each account, how many active deals are there, and how much are they worth? This shows clearly the potential business that has been identified and developed by the salesperson. Regardless of how big an account is currently, if the salesperson has been actively calling on it, the salesperson should have identified at least some potential business to pursue.

Sales Calls

We look at both the calls that have been made to date and how many are currently planned for the future. These numbers are likely to be all over the place, and what is good or bad will vary depending on the exact nature of your business. What you are always looking for here is balance. If an account is in a salesperson's portfolio, then it should be actively called on, and there should always be a plan for at least one upcoming call. Customers with the most volume or opportunity will certainly have more calls than ones with less, but you should see a reasonable correlation there.

Account-Plan Tactics

Every account plan should include some minimum number of tactics to be executed on during the year. This view allows you to see how those tactics are progressing, and accounts that have seen little or no progress on that front will be very clear to you. As with other activities here, if an account is worth including in the salesperson's portfolio, then he or she should be actively driving a planned set of tactics.

Last Touch

This is an indication of the last time the salesperson has edited either the account record, the account plan, an opportunity tied to it, or a sales call on it. You can pick a timeframe, but if a salesperson has not touched a customer in some way in the past thirty days, you have to ask yourself why it is included in the portfolio of accounts.

Keep in mind that if the sales manager is not careful with how he or she conducts the conversation around this report, it can start to feel a lot more like inspection than coaching. A manager needs to view the items above like a filter to see where there might be issues on which he or she can guide the salesperson through coaching.

The sales manager is looking for two big things here. Is the salesperson's activity appropriately balanced across the account portfolio, and is the salesperson being proactive enough in the approaches to the accounts?

If it looks like activity is out of balance, the manager needs to ask the salesperson what he or she thinks about that. Is there some reason that is driving it? Is there anything that the sales manager can do to help the salesperson rebalance it? What kind of opportunities are being missed in the accounts that are not getting as much attention?

If the manager does not see proactive approaches in which the salesperson is driving something rather than just reacting, then the manager needs to ask provocative questions of the salesperson to lead him or her to the same conclusion. The manager should also be probing for anything to do that could help free up the salesperson to be more proactive.

That kind of coaching will require some real patience, but it will make a huge difference in how the coaching sessions are received.

Keeping notes during this session is critical—the sales manager does not want to make the salespeople repeat themselves from week to week. The manager can keep notes in all kinds of tools, but I have found that in the case of pipeline coaching, it can be most effective to keep the notes right in the deals themselves. An example of an object that you can embed in the opportunity section of your CRM for this is shown in chapter 3-4.

The real measure of success for these meetings is whether or not the salespeople actually look forward to them. If they get upset with their managers when they have to reschedule structured-coaching sessions, then the managers are doing something right. If they end up dreading the meetings, then the sales managers need to rethink their approaches.

Joint Sales Calls

Through joint sales calls, managers get to know their salespeople the best. They see them with their customers while they are actively selling. They talk about their planning before the call and debrief on their thinking and next steps afterward. Their observations of these items are going to tell them far more about the salespeople and the customers than any after-action reporting. Joint sales calls are also some of the most delicate meetings for sales managers to navigate, particularly if they don't want to make the mistakes that Joe made at the beginning of this chapter. What makes them delicate is deciding how actively involved they should be during the call itself. That is going to depend on just how the meetings were set up.

There are three classic setups for joint calls that I like to call the ride along, the customer request, and the business-card leapfrog.

The Ride Along

The ride-along call is the classic joint call. The manager is following the salesperson around for some period of time to see him or her in action and to get a sense of what is going on in the market.

I like to call these "Hi, how ya doing?" calls. They can have real value for the sales manager, but typically they require the salesperson to make a withdrawal on their goodwill bank with the customer. It's a bit of a necessary evil, but if it is not combined with good coaching, then it is a waste of the manager's time, the salesperson's time, and the customer's goodwill.

The manager's main job in this call is to observe. The manager is there to see how good the salesperson is with the customer and to hear firsthand from the customer about how their business is going and how well your company is supporting it. This should be a very active observation where the manager is taking notes both on what the customer is saying as well as any coachable moments from the salesperson's conduct of the call to follow up afterward.

In the course of the meeting, the manager should certainly engage – the trick is to what degree to do it without taking over the call. The manager should ask questions of the customer and might even pitch some element of what the company can do for the customer.

However, this has to be done with some balance to ensure that the lines of demarcation are clear—the salesperson owns the relationship. A good rule of thumb is that at the end of the meeting, the salesperson should have done 80 percent of the talking for your company, and the manager should have done 20 percent.

The follow-up coaching with the salesperson is particularly important. Ideally, this should be done immediately after the sales call while you drive away or are getting coffee or a meal. Once again, questions need to drive this session, not lectures. An ideal form of this for the manager would be along these lines:

> How do you think that the call went overall?
>
> What are your biggest takeaways from the meeting?
>
> What else were you looking for in the meeting?
>
> Can you give me some feedback on how I did in the call? How well did I meet your needs?
>
> What help do you need from me to meet the commitments made in the meeting?

During the meeting, you asked the customer about X. What was your thought process there?

Are there any movements during the meeting that you want to go back and do over? Why?

What do you think is your most important next step from this meeting? Why?

If you could write the sales-call plan again, what would you have done differently?

The Customer Request

The customer request was set up because the customer specifically wanted to meet with the manager, most typically to discuss a problem. Chances are that the manager is going to have a starring role in the meeting. That being said, the manager still needs to work actively to keep the salesperson in the dialogue—the salesperson is still the primary owner of the relationship after the sales call is over.

This can be touchy to manage. I will never forget one such call when we sat down with the salesperson directly across from the customer and me to the customer's right. The customer kicked off the meeting and promptly picked up his chair, turned it ninety degrees to directly face me, and said, "So…you're the guy."

At the end of the day, the manager has to deal with whatever the situation is, commit to solving the problem, and make whatever apologies are needed. It should always be clear that although the manager will be engaged to help solve the problem, the salesperson will be the lead on it. This does not mean that the manager cuts off communication after the meeting; the manager certainly wants the relationship. The manager just has to be careful to enhance—rather than supplant—the salesperson's relationship.

The follow-up coaching here is similar to the questions above but has some additional questions for the manager to help set up future communications:

> What issues do you see for us meeting these commitments? What can I do to help you get them done?
>
> How satisfied do you think the customer was with the meeting? What else do you think that we have to do to follow up?
>
> What kind of follow-up communication do you want me to send to the customer?

The Business-Card Leapfrog

The business-card leapfrog is one of my all-time favorites—primarily because this is the sales call that your salesperson specifically wanted the manager along on. This comes when a salesperson has been working to penetrate a customer but can't get above a certain level. The offer of a meeting with a manager of the appropriate level is used to get a meeting with a higher-level person at the customer's site.

As with the customer-request call, the manager is going to need to balance ongoing communication with this customer to ensure that the salesperson is getting the bulk of it. By doing this, the manager has leveraged the managerial position to help the salesperson gain a relationship with someone who normally would not have even taken a meeting with him or her.

Once the door to that meeting has been opened, the salesperson needs to be coached on how to take the relationship forward. The link that the manager has built should be maintained, but the salesperson needs to be moved into the primary position. The manager's coaching questions need to help the salesperson set the specific strategy of how this will be done.

> What kind of follow-up communication do you want me to send to the customer?
>
> Now that we have met X, where should we be headed next? Why?

In any of these scenarios, the manager's main role is to listen. The manager's main objectives are to observe the salesperson and back him or her. Before the call, it is critical that everyone participating in it is aware of and agrees to the plan. We discuss this in much greater depth in chapter 2-5.

<u>Ad-Hoc Coaching</u>

Once sales managers are clear on what a coaching mind-set is, it will become a habit to be in a question-based dialogue when reviewing joint sales calls or holding structured-coaching sessions. The harder task will be getting themselves to change gears when the phone rings and salespeople put them on the spot with situations that they need help with.

This is a moment, particularly since the manager is likely to be busy with something else, that the manager is likely to slip into problem-solving mode and just tell the salesperson what to do. Therefore, this is where a manager needs to develop a conditioned reflex to go to what I think of as the most powerful coaching question of all:

> What do you think that we should do?

You will be amazed how often the salesperson is going to have an answer coming right away. This is natural. He or she knows the situation and the customer's needs, so the salesperson probably knows what can best be done to handle things. What the salesperson is often looking for in that moment is either permission from the manager to do that thing or help from the manager to get the organization to do it.

This does not mean that the manager's role is just to blindly do what is asked. Once the idea is out there, the manager should act as both a sounding board and a devil's advocate.

Why is this the best thing to do?

What other way might we do the same thing?

What is the downside to taking this approach?

Managers need to be careful when they do this. They are not trying to shut the conversation down; they are trying to flesh the idea out and look at it from multiple directions. Over time, the salespeople will come to trust their managers with these lines of questioning, but in the beginning, they can view it as managers attacking their ideas.

Some of the best training that I ever had on this came from Bill Wallace at Revenue Storm. After going through their coaching class, they reinforced the material with fly-on-the-wall sessions where Bill observed me actually coaching my salespeople.

We had just finished one of these sessions in which he had observed me coaching one of my salespeople on a deal for over an hour. He asked me how I was feeling, and I told him that I felt completely exhausted. His response? "Great! That's how you know that you are doing it right."

A real coaching session requires a significant level of mental intensity. The manager has to be in an active-listening mode the entire time and monitoring him or herself to ensure adherence to a question-based dialogue. Over time, this gets a bit easier, but at first, a manager will find it to be quite draining. The good news is that if the session is going well and the manager is really solving the problem, there is an offset that comes from how energized the manager and the salesperson can get as they come up with the right answers—together.

KEY TAKEAWAYS:

* The primary role of any sales manager is to act as a coach for the team. The amount of time spent coaching should reflect that.
* Coaching is not micromanagement or inspection—it is using Socratic questioning to help the salesperson solve problems.
* The coaching of salespeople will range from regular, structured-coaching sessions to joint sales calls to ad-hoc coaching sessions—all of which need to be carefully managed to stay in the "coaching" mode.

Chapter 1-5

Cleaning Out the Deadwood

One of the toughest parts of any manager's job is dealing with performance issues. It's never fun to have the adult conversations that this requires. However, as tough as it is to do, it's also one of the most important parts of the job—particularly for sales managers.

> I'm working with Ethan, one of the managers on my team. Ethan is a first-time manager, and he's never had to deal with a performance problem before, but he is up against a wall with Peter, a long-time employee.
>
> Peter had always been pretty solid but lately had not been putting that much effort into things. Ethan had had several conversations with him about it, but things had just not been getting better at all.
>
> To make matters worse, Peter was a great guy. We had both known him for over a decade and really liked him. It was going to be a tough conversation, and Ethan had no idea how to have it in a way that was not going to turn very negative.
>
> Putting someone on a performance plan and having a frank conversation is never easy, and it sure as heck is never easy for the employee to

hear. We decided to sit down together with Peter to have the performance conversation.

Peter came in and, after we told him what was going on, was clearly shocked. He had no idea at all that his performance was lacking, and we could tell that he was having a hard time processing it.

"So, this is really just a way for you to build up official documentation to fire me, isn't it?"

"Peter, if we wanted to fire you, then HR would be in here, and we would have already done it. We've got plenty of documentation to do that. The point of this conversation is that we *don't* want to fire you."

"So why the formal plan then?"

"Peter, think of it this way. We are out in the middle of the ocean, and you are in the water drowning. This plan is a rope that we are throwing you from a boat. The trick is that we can't just pull you back into the boat. You have to swim to the rope, you have to grab onto the rope, and you have to pull yourself back into the boat. We don't want you to drown at all, but we can only do so much; you have to do the biggest part."

Peter was still a bit shell shocked, as anyone would be, and we asked him to take the rest of the day off and reflect.

The first thing the next morning, Peter was in my office with Ethan.

"You know, I thought a lot about what you guys said yesterday, and I have to admit, I was pretty pissed at you, but the more that I thought about it, the more I realized that it's up to me to fix this, and I am here to tell you that you are not going to need ninety days to see me improve. I'm going to be off this plan in sixty."

The best part of the story? He was off the plan in thirty days.

What we saw here was one of three classic reactions to conversations about poor performance that I have observed over the years. I call it the "bucket of ice water." Peter genuinely had no idea that his performance was off track; he'd had conversations leading up to it, but none of them really registered. It took the toughest conversation with a formal performance plan on the table to wake him up—just like pouring a bucket of ice water on his head. Once he was truly aware of the issues and the seriousness, he was back on track almost immediately.

Folks in this category almost inevitably succeed in getting back on track and, like Peter, often do so well ahead of the plan schedule. They generally don't need skill improvement; they just need to recalibrate on aspects of what they are doing and make adjustments using coaching feedback from their managers. Performance issues like this normally arise when the person has other things going on in life that take over the person's awareness.

I call the second classic reaction the "Oh, yeah? I'll show you." The people in this group don't wake up from the news that there are performance issues. Instead, they actually end up going even deeper down the rabbit hole of poor performance. They are so convinced that they are right and you are wrong that they actually start to amplify everything that you told them was a negative behavior in some kind of perverse attempt to prove you wrong.

Sadly, people with this reaction often exit the performance plan early as well—via termination. In trying to show up management and prove their cases, they end up doing something that is actionable. I absolutely hate this type of case as the only good thing about the outcome is that a problem has been removed from the team.

You have to be vigilant when managing a plan for someone with this reaction. While the improvement plan is proceeding, things can get messy—particularly with the other salespeople, channel partners, and customers around them. The trick here is to recognize when things are going in a negative direction and take decisive action before too much damage is done. Waiting around is not going to make it better.

The final classic reaction is the toughest one to deal with. I call it the "okeydokey." The people in this category nod their heads and comply with everything at the bare minimum levels required to keep their jobs but never really change.

The "okeydokey" people will finish the plans on schedule, but you often find yourself wanting to extend them at the end as you really have not seen marked changes in behavior. Inevitably, you are going to end up putting them back on new plans a short time later. These are often the "nice guys" whom you like well enough, making them even harder to deal with.

Deal with them you must. Letting weak-to-mediocre performers hang around sends a terrible message to the rest of the organization. Nothing demoralizes top performers more than watching weak ones hang on year after year while the team makes quota only if the top performers cover for them.

More fundamentally, this is not fair to the weak performers themselves. Most of the salespeople that you will see in this category are at that level because, at the end of the day, they are not really salespeople.

This may seem cold, but it is one of the brutal facts of running a sales team. No amount of coaching is going to make someone who is not really a salesperson any better than a mediocre performer. The best favor that you can do for that person is to help them to realize that he or she is not really a salesperson. You will do far more good by helping that person look for a job that is much more suitable to who they really are.

You owe it to both the salesperson and organization to take decisive action.

One of the biggest issues that I have with the topic of performance improvement is that it normally centers completely around the performance-improvement plan, or PIP. PIPs are necessary and important tools, but I've seen far too many cases where the approach to performance management is to go from zero to "Fix this in ninety days, or you are fired" in just one step.

If we are doing our jobs properly as managers, our approaches to performance management should consist of progressive steps. The hard truth in Peter's case at the beginning of the chapter was that Ethan failed him in some ways—he never should have been shocked when he found out that he was going on a PIP. He should have been well aware of his own performance issues, and different coaching actions should have already taken place long before the PIP conversation. Ethan liked Peter so much that he never could bring himself to have the tough conversations with him.

This is particularly true in sales. Salespeople always know their numbers, and the best of them will beat up on themselves far more when they are missing them than any manager ever will. However, a PIP in sales should never be just about the numbers—at least not the short-term ones. There are a lot of perfectly valid reasons for a salesperson to be missing numbers in one period or other. The performance issues come in when it's not just the result that is in question but also the underlying behaviors, competencies, actions, or compliance with policies that are of issue as well.

If you are in the process of trying to rebuild or redirect a sales team, you can get a lot of those cases. If there is one thing that salespeople have in spades it's inertia. Once a salesperson finds what works for them, they stick with it. Convincing salespeople to change is hard and requires consistent commitment from managers to perpetually reinforce the new direction. This is where a properly designed coaching plan or PIP can really help.

Without a doubt, this is the hardest part of any manager's job. Nobody likes having these conversations, and only a sadist would enjoy telling people that their jobs are on the line. However, this is also one of the most important parts of the manager's job. Making sure that you have the right people on the team and that the people there are performing is central to anything else that you are going to do.

As you lead up to taking formal action, there should be plenty of informal coaching conversations as part of normal, day-to-day sales management. It's when we find that those conversations are not having an impact or are not really being heard by the salesperson that we need to take things to the next level.

As part of this progressive approach, before going all the way to a PIP, you can have a slightly less formal coaching plan put in place to see if that is enough to get things back on track with the salesperson. Coaching plans give some structure to the process but don't create the same emotional issues that a PIP is inevitably going to.

In both cases, it is important to keep the right balance between activities and results. A plan that is just a list of goals to meet is not really designed to help the salesperson improve—it's really just putting the salesperson on notice to figure out how to improve by themselves. To go back to the story at the start of the chapter, we should at least be throwing them the rope. The best improvement plans have sets of activities that are designed to put salespeople back on the right paths toward meeting those results.

Coaching Plans

Coaching plans are intended to get the salesperson to focus on some of the core concepts that have gone off track. The design of a coaching plan is twofold: you want to set up a basis for an ongoing dialogue with the sales manager, and you want to create some activities that will force the salesperson to step back and look at the situation more objectively. As the coaching plan is intended to be a relatively quick and somewhat informal course correction, it is based on a sixty-day timeframe instead of the more traditional ninety days.

It's best to get the plan off the ground with a one-on-one meeting between the manager and the salesperson. Some companies might really want to have HR in the room, but I would advise against it. The intent in having the coaching plan as kind of a lower-level PIP is to give the manager a way to start a serious dialogue with the salesperson without having to go to the extent of a formal PIP.

In the one-on-one meeting, the manager should explain exactly that and emphasize that the intent is to create a series of specific coaching conversations with the manager that will help to get the salesperson back on track.

The messaging should be along the lines of this letter. Depending on the culture of your company, you may or may not actually use the letter, but it does well to accompany the written coaching plan when you send it to the salesperson.

> Dear Salesperson,
>
> As we have discussed, your performance as a salesperson needs some help to get back to the level that we expect in this organization. In order to help you correct this, we have created a sixty-day coaching plan for you.
>
> The intent of this plan is simple: it will zero you in on some specific issues with your performance and create coaching dialogues between you and me that can best illustrate the specific gaps that I am seeing.
>
> The details of the plan are attached below.

Please take this opportunity to step back and reflect on what you have been doing and, even more importantly, not doing as a sales professional. A coaching plan can only work if you genuinely recognize its need and fully embrace its intent.

As your manager, I will help to coach you through this, but it is entirely up to you to make the changes in behavior, activities, and approach that will result in your successful completion of the plan.

Sincerely,

Manager

If you are trying to take a team in the direction suggested by this book, a basic coaching plan would look like the one below. It assumes that the requirements and expectations for the use of your CRM tool have been clearly communicated to the team and are compiled in a playbook for reference.

Day 1

Use our CRM software proactively in all of your sales activities. Be ready to pass a random audit at any given time—at least one will be conducted per month. All CRM information is to be current at all times starting no later than day 3.

By Day 10

Review the CRM playbook in detail, and discuss any questions with your manager in a coaching session by day 20. Be prepared to self-identify your most significant gaps in the use of our CRM and how you will be modifying your activities to address them.

By Day 20

Submit a basic sales plan to your manager, laying out all of your accounts and containing concise answers for following elements:

* What does the account do?
* What is the account's application for our product?
* What is your strategy for the account?
* What are the four major tactical objectives (with dates) that you need to accomplish in a year to make your strategy work?

  This will be reviewed and discussed with your manager in a coaching session by day 30.

By Day 30

Read *Hope Is Not a Strategy*, by Rick Page. Send a brief summary to your manager by day 30 of the plan with bullet points of the most important things that you learned from the book and how you will change your daily activity and overall sales approach as a result. This will be reviewed and discussed with your manager in a coaching session by day 40.

By Day 40

Read *The Checklist Manifesto*, by Atul Gawande. Send a brief summary to your manager by day 40 with bullet points of the most important things that you learned from the book and how you will change your daily activity as a result. This will be reviewed and discussed with your manager in a coaching session by day 50.

By Day 50

Prepare a brief summary for your manager with bullet points detailing the most significant learnings that you have had during your coaching plan and how you think your behavior and style as a salesperson will differ going forward. Send this summary to your manager for a coaching session to be held prior to day 60.

The first two requirements are pretty basic; you really are just trying to formally get the salesperson back to doing two of the most basic things that are already in the job description—using the CRM system and having solid plans for all accounts.

Notice that this is not about the sales that may result from the activities. Using a coaching plan, we just want to get the salesperson back to proper execution of the fundamentals. There is an assumption that you are using some kind of a playbook that details how you expect your team to use the CRM.

The two reading assignments and "book reports" serve a very different purpose. You may be shaking your head right now at the concept, but please bear with me for a moment.

The idea here is to get the salesperson to step back from the minutiae of your business and think about a theoretical issue that is behind what we are trying to do with the sales team, not to get him or her to write a college thesis. The intent of the written summary—and the requirement for bullet points—is just to get the person to think a bit deeper as he or she reads and to set up some meaningful structure to the conversations to come.

The main point of the summary is to set up a dialogue with the manager about what the salesperson thought about the book. That dialogue is where the real coaching is going to take place. Personally, I think that these two books serve a particular purpose, but you should feel free to change them out if you have other books that illustrate your sales philosophy better. The dialogue is the important part.

Hope Is Not a Strategy was a bit like a *Dilbert* cartoon for me the first time that I read it. I could swear that Rick Page had worked in my company as a salesperson. He was so spot on with the issues that we were dealing with. It was then that I realized, just as with Scott Adams's *Dilbert* cartoons, these issues were universal. Since then, I've suggested this book to every salesperson and sales manager that I have worked with.

The book lays out a solid process for handling complex, consultative selling as a team builds and then executes a strategy to penetrate accounts. It's a solid approach that puts the emphasis on the salesperson taking control instead of just waiting around to see what happens. As we discussed in chapter 1-2, that "initiative" characteristic is central to what makes a true salesperson.

The coaching conversations around the book should focus on that topic. As the manager talks about whatever specific element that the salesperson wants to bring out from the book, he or she can steer the conversation there and get a real sense of how the salesperson thinks personally about it. It's not only a great way to reinforce the concepts that are important to your sales approach, but it's also going to give the manager some real insight into how the salesperson thinks about selling.

At the end of the day, if the manager can't make the light bulb go on over the salesperson's head about the importance of taking initiative and being proactive, then there is going to be a real problem going forward that will have to be dealt with.

A large part of the process that we discuss later in this book involves the use of checklists. *The Checklist Manifesto* was one of the drivers of this approach. In the book, Atul Gawande lays out an excellent case for the use of checklists beyond just the traditional examples like that of an airline pilot.

I've always found the resistance to the checklist approach interesting. The most common response that I get to the suggestion of using a checklist before, say, going on a sales call is "I've been doing this for twenty years; I don't need a checklist. I know what to do."

I like to counter with the fact that my brother Eric has been flying jet aircraft for over thirty-five years, and he still uses a checklist for just about everything that he does on the aircraft. Why? Because keeping that aircraft safe is the most important things that a pilot does.

Now, nobody is going to die if a salesperson messes up a sales call, but if the sales call is the single most important thing that a salesperson does (and, in my opinion, it is), then why wouldn't he or she use a simple checklist just to be sure that everything is covered?

Think back on that salesperson saying, "I've been doing this for twenty years, I don't need a checklist. I know what to do." I can't tell you how many times I have walked out of a call with one of them and found out that the salesperson forgot to get something done. That's OK; it's human for forget things, especially in a tense sales call. That's why checklists were invented.

The coaching conversations about this book should focus on the benefits that checklists have brought in other professions in the book's examples. From there, you can migrate to some brainstorming about other aspects of your sales environment or business that might benefit from a basic checklist and what elements might be on the checklist.

Keep in mind, we are not talking about crazy, complex checklists here that just serve some bureaucratic goal or to run reports on. We are talking about simple, short checklists that help to plan and execute a better sales call.

By the end of the conversation, you are looking to see if the salesperson's eyes have genuinely opened up about the benefits to adding the discipline of checklists to their approach.

Again, while I really like the dialogue that comes out of these two books in particular, you don't have to use just these. You can use any books that suit your purposes and sales style. The real point is the coaching conversations that they drive with the salesperson.

During the coaching plan, the manager should also continue to have the normal structured-coaching sessions that we discussed earlier. Since this is just a sixty-day coaching plan, if the interval is not already weekly, you should consider increasing the frequency to that rate. For a coaching plan to be effective, you need to touch base with the salesperson as frequently as is reasonable.

The final item in the plan is a one-on-one meeting between the manager and the salesperson that hopefully concludes the coaching plan. One key thing in this meeting is that the salesperson needs to do most of the talking, not the manager. The manager needs to be ready with open-ended questions to draw out what the salesperson has learned and has changed.

You want the salesperson to tell the manager, unprompted, how he or she is going to be acting differently going forward as a result of the coaching plan. Until the manager hears that clearly, the manager should just be asking open-ended questions to draw it out.

If the manager does not hear that message of change, then it's clear that the coaching plan did not work and that a full performance-improvement plan is needed.

Performance-Improvement Plans

If normal coaching and a coaching plan have not been sufficient to turn a salesperson around, or if the performance is bad enough to warrant it, then the best course of action left is a formal performance-improvement plan. The difference between this and the coaching plan is that you are making it clear to the salesperson that if performance does not turn around by the end of the PIP, he or she will be terminated.

As we discussed earlier, this meeting should hardly be a surprise to any of the parties involved. There should have been enough conversations ahead of time that the salesperson knows that there are serious issues with performance. Unlike the coaching plan, it is highly advised to have an HR representative involved in the meeting and to be available to speak individually with the salesperson afterward if he or she would like.

It's hard to keep this meeting from coming off as adversarial, but it needs to be done. If the manager can't get across that the intent of this plan is to help the salesperson, then it ends up just being a formality on the path to firing them.

The manager needs to find a way to communicate this in a way that matches the manager's personal style and relationship with the salesperson, but something along the lines of the dialogue at the beginning of this chapter can serve as a road map.

When the manager gives the salesperson a copy of the PIP, a cover letter emphasizing the same points should go along with it. Here is a suggested template for that.

> Dear Salesperson,
>
> As we have discussed, your performance as a salesperson has been below the level that is acceptable in this organization. In order to help you correct this, we have created a ninety-day performance-improvement plan for you.
>
> The intent of this plan is simple: it will take you back to the fundamentals of selling and create coaching dialogues between you and me that can best illustrate the specific gaps that you have in your performance.
>
> The details of the plan are attached below.
>
> It is critical that you fully complete every element of this plan. Failure to complete the plan successfully over the next ninety days will result in actions up to and including the termination of your employment. We will document and discuss your completion as you progress, and it is my sincere hope that you will finish this plan back on track as a salesperson.

Please take this opportunity to step back and reflect on what you have been doing and, even more importantly, not doing as a sales professional. A performance plan can only work if you genuinely recognize its need and fully embrace its intent.

As your manager, I will help to coach you through this, but it is entirely up to you to make the changes that will result in your successful completion of the plan.

Sincerely,

Manager

The PIP itself should look something like what is shown below. Everything needs to be laid out as a traditional SMART objective (specific, measurable, achievable, realistic, and time based). Several of these same elements are in the coaching plan—this just takes things to a level appropriate to the serious nature of the PIP.

While it is appropriate to include expectations of financial results in the PIP, the bulk of the content should be about the activities that are going to help the salesperson to better deliver those results.

Day 1

Starting immediately, make at least ten sales calls per week, properly planned and followed up on in our CRM tool. Send a weekly report on your sales calls to your manager every Friday by 5:00 p.m. per the following template:

* List the sales calls that you made this past week with links to each event plan in the CRM.
* Indicate any sales calls that were with new customers.

* List any new opportunities that were developed from your sales calls this week along with links to the opportunities in the CRM.
* List the most significant follow-up tasks coming from your sales calls this week and any help that you are asking for to get them accomplished.
* List any opportunities moved closer to closed-won this week, and indicate what moved them forward as well as your next actionable step on the opportunity. (Provide links to each opportunity discussed.)
* List the must-discuss items for your next one-on-one coaching session with your manager.
* List the sales calls that you plan to make next week with links to each event plan in the CRM.

Use the CRM proactively in all of your sales activities. Be ready to pass a random audit at any given time—at least one will be conducted per month. All CRM information is to be current at all times starting no later than day 3 of the PIP.

By Day 10

Submit a written self-assessment of your own performance as a salesperson to your manager. At a minimum, this assessment should include your reasons for your poor performance to date, the primary skills that you feel you need to improve, and your own plan to improve those skills over the ninety days of the plan. This plan will be reviewed with your manager in a coaching session by day 15, combined with your manager's input, and tracked for the period of the PIP.

By Day 20

Submit a detailed sales plan to your manager, laying out all of your accounts and containing at least the following elements:

* What does the account do?
* What is the account's application for our product?
* What is your strategy for the account?
* What are the four major tactical objectives (with dates) that you need to accomplish in a year to make your strategy work?
* Prior year sales, planned sales for this year.

This will be reviewed and discussed with your manager in a coaching session by day 30.

By Day 30

Read *Never Fly Solo*, by Waldo Waldman. Send a brief written summary to your manager in bullet format by day 40 of the most important things that you learned from the book and how you think you should adjust your approach to teamwork as a result. Lay out anything in the book that you disagree with or think does not apply to our business along with your reasons why. This will be reviewed and discussed with your manager in a coaching session by day 40.

By Day 40

Complete an in-depth analysis of one of your accounts, agreed to by your manager, using publicly available financial information and presenting your conclusions as to what the primary financial drivers inside that account are and how you should adjust your sales approach accordingly. This will be reviewed and discussed with your manager in a coaching session by day 50.

By Day 50

Pick a product in your portfolio, and prepare a pitch to sell that product based on a real financial value that it will deliver to a specific customer. Send the pitch to your manager to be discussed in a coaching session by day 60.

By Day 60

Conduct at least one joint sales call with your manager. Schedule and manage a precall planning session with your manager. At a minimum, the plan should include:

* What do you want to accomplish in the sales call?
* What information do you need to get from the customer?
    * Who is responsible for getting each piece of information?
* What information do you need to give to the customer?
    * Who is responsible for giving each piece of information?
* What do you need to be ready for in the meeting?

Review the outcome in a coaching session to be held no more than one day after the sales call.

By Day 80

Prepare a written summary for your manager detailing the most significant learnings that you have had during your PIP and how you think your behavior and style as a salesperson will differ going forward. Send to your manager for a coaching session to be held prior to day 90.

There are two key psychological elements in play here. First of all, before the salesperson can improve, he or she must admit the issues with nonperformance. This needs to be in the salesperson's own words, not the manager's, and that is the intent of the written self-assessment.

Secondly, there are a lot of very basic tasks here that any experienced salesperson is likely to find humiliating. The intent here is not at all to humiliate but to force him or her to get back to those basics. Chances are that with the current state of the performance, the person has gone far astray on those basics. The manager can use judgment on the need for each of these elements on a case-by-case basis, but I would not remove them lightly.

As with the coaching plan, the main intent of all of the items here is to drive a dialogue in the coaching sessions with the managers. Simply reviewing the output of the basic tasks in the weekly reports or the sales plan will uncover any basic competency gaps and allow the manager to address them. More importantly, those conversations will give the manager insight into how the salesperson thinks about the whole selling process and allow for appropriate adjustments to coaching.

The book *Never Fly Solo* is about teamwork. A lot of salespeople like to think of themselves as lone rangers, out on the front lines alone. We all know that is not the case. The very best salespeople leverage a huge network of resources from within their companies and their channels. The key realization that they have is that while they might certainly be capable of performing task X or task Y, there are other resources that can do it better or more effectively. Their job is to handle their specialty—selling.

Waldo Waldman does a great job of relating what he learned as a fighter pilot to the business world. He goes back to the very real environment that he lived in, in which he literally put his life in the hands of his wingman so that he could focus 100 percent on achieving his part of the mission. Although life and death are hardly on the line in this case, an effective salesperson has to do the same thing by trusting sales support, inside sales, operations, manufacturing, and services resources, just to name a few.

The coaching on this book can get very specific by just walking through the list of things that the salesperson did that week that were not directly related to making sales calls or closing deals. When you talk about those tasks, you can ask the open-ended question about which other resources in the organization might have been able to do those tasks instead. Ultimately, the salesperson has to show that he or she not only will engage other parts of the organization, but that it will be insisted upon.

As with the coaching plans – the exact book that you chose to use is not as important as the coaching conversations that it should drive. The three books that I have mentioned serve specific purposes that may or may not fit well with what you are trying to accomplish with your overall sales team or what you are specifically trying to correct with an individual salesperson. In my experience, troubled salespeople often need help with one or more of these three things.

Hope Is Not a Strategy is intended to drive conversations around selling.

The Checklist Manifesto is intended to drive conversations around process.

Never Fly Solo is intended to drive conversations around teamwork.

The in-depth account analysis task is valuable with or without a PIP being done and should be targeted at a top account. The intent is to see if the salesperson is able to look at the annual report and financial filings of a customer and discern what the larger business issues are inside the account. This is a test of both the salesperson's ability to think beyond the traditional feature-benefits selling model and their ability to think strategically about an account.

As with all of our items here, the real benefit is going to come during the coaching conversations with the salesperson. The manager needs to let the salesperson do most of the talking and stick to using probing questions as discussed in chapter 1-4.

If the customer base is made up of smaller customers who might not have public financial filings, the exercise can be modified to be based on what the salesperson does know about the customer from contact with them.

The trick here is to be sure that the drivers around which the sales strategy is designed are not based on what purchasing or engineering may be saying, but on the true financial priorities of the company's leader or the market drivers that the salesperson knows will impact the customer.

The next task in the plan is having the salesperson put together a finance-based pitch. We all know that the world of feature-benefit selling is long in the past. The higher that you try to sell in any organization, the more the story has to relate back to a real-dollar impact that your product or solution is going to have for the customer. Having the salesperson put this together for you is going to show you clearly whether he or she has this capability.

As you coach and question the salesperson afterward, you will get an excellent sense of the thought process that was used in putting it together and whether the salesperson was able to view his or her solution through the customer's eyes.

The joint sales call can take place at any time during the PIP; it just should be done by day 60. The manager should use his or her own judgment on how many calls and what type of customer they want to see the salesperson interact with. If time allows, it can be ideal to do one early in the PIP and then one late in the PIP to see if there has been any real improvement in planning or execution in response to coaching from the first call. This is one of the more important activities for the manager. There is no hiding on a sales call, and the manager will see all of the salesperson's skills (and deficiencies) on display in these calls.

Finally, we come to the summary meeting at the end of the PIP. This is a critical period as you have to make the toughest of decisions here. Has this salesperson gotten back on track, and will he or she stay there, or has the time come for termination? There is no way that you can take this decision lightly, but you also have to be ready to be brutally honest with yourself. Every weak performer that you allow in your organization has to be made up for by someone else.

What you are looking for:

* Every task should have been completed on or ahead of schedule.

* The salesperson should have taken the initiative to get every coaching session on your calendar right at the start of the PIP.
* After the initial shock of starting the PIP, the salesperson needs to have shown a genuine humility; he or she should recognize and accept that performance needed to be improved.
* The coaching sessions should all have ended on a positive note. Even if there was philosophical disagreement over some point from the books or tasks, both of you should have left feeling like you had just had a great conversation about the art and profession of selling and that progress had been made.

Red Flags:

* If the salesperson did not attack every task in the PIP proactively, or if you had to chase him or her down to get anything done on time, there is a problem. The person did not take seriously the message that his or her job depended on the PIP.
* If there is any element of the coaching conversations that showed you this is not someone who is dedicated to the art and profession of selling, then you have to admit that this is not truly a salesperson. If it is just a job to this person, then what is he or she really going to do for you?
* If there is any doubt in your mind that the person is going to get the job done, listen to it.

None of this is going to be easy, but it is incredibly necessary. Sales teams have never been able to afford to carry a large number of weak salespeople, and in today's world, you can only afford to have true salespeople. The intent of the coaching plans and PIPs is to help you get a faltering salesperson back on track and to confirm for you that he or she is the kind of salesperson that you want in your organization.

If someone is not, stop kidding yourself, and move that person out.

KEY TAKEAWAYS:

* Nobody likes having the tough performance conversations, but they are one of the most important parts of a manager's job.
* Nothing discourages top performers like watching poor performance be unaddressed.
* There are three classic responses to a performance plan that all have to be managed differently:

  1. "Bucket of ice water."
  2. "Oh, yeah? I'll show you."
  3. "Okeydokey."

* Sales performance is not just about the numbers; it also has to be about behaviors, activities, and underlying competencies.
* Performance management needs to be progressive, from feedback sessions to coaching plans to performance-improvement plans.
* Once you have reached the end of a PIP and the problems are not fixed, stop kidding yourself and take action.

Chapter 1-6

Freeing Up the Salesperson

Have you ever met a sales manager who would not gladly take additional salespeople for his or her team? Have you ever met one who was happy when headcount is lost on their team?

Every sales manager knows that the more salespeople that they have, the easier it is to generate revenue. Despite that fact, sometimes we don't think about all of the activities that effectively take salespeople off our teams by taking up time that keeps them away from their customers.

> We are having the first meeting of global leadership for a commercial organization that has just recently been formed. Two adjacent sales teams were being brought together to offer a more complete solution for our customers.
>
> All of the sales, sales support, and marketing leaders from around the world were brought in for this kickoff and filled up a giant meeting room in Atlanta on a crisp day in early spring.
>
> I was going to be leading the largest region, and my boss asked me to talk to the larger group about the philosophy behind what I wanted to do with my team.

Although on the surface it had nothing to do with sales, I decided to tell a story about the formation of Southwest Airlines, citing a great book by Kevin and Jackie Freiberg called *Nuts!*.

"To give you an idea about how I want to think about this sales team, I'm going to tell you a story about how a major American airline called Southwest got started. The airline was founded by a man named Herb Kelleher. Herb had absolutely no background in aviation when he started the airline, but he had a critical insight into how the money really came in to the business.

"Herb realized that when you got down to it, all of the money was generated by the airplanes and that the only time that they were making any money was when they were in the air. If the plane was sitting on the tarmac or at the gate, it was not making money.

"Herb and his team focused the design of their entire business model around this fact. They standardized the airline with just one type of aircraft so that all of the pilots could fly any plane in the fleet and any mechanic could work on any one as well. They set up labor contracts to ensure that everyone could help 'turn' the plane when it was at the gate. They designed a unique boarding process that eliminated seat assignments to ensure that passengers got on the plane as quickly as possible.

"The result? Southwest was able to turn a plane in thirty minutes while it took their competitors over two hours. That gave their revenue-generating asset that much more time to make money than their competitors had.

"What we have to realize here is that our salespeople are our airplanes. Anything that they are doing that does not directly tie to selling makes us less competitive."

When I finished my talk, Sheila, the head of our sales-support organization came up to me to talk.

"You just gave me our new mission statement: 'Our job is to keep the planes in the air.'"

My favorite part of what came next was how the measurement system for sales support changed. After that meeting, the primary measure of the support organization became how many sales calls a week the salespeople were making. What a great example of collaboration! The sales-support team members recognized that if they were doing their jobs right, the result would be more time in front of customers for the salespeople.

That attitude of focus on "keeping the planes in the air" is what this chapter is all about. How do we ensure that we are setting up the sales organization in such a way that we maximize how much time the sales team gets to sell? How do we give them the tools to do it as effectively as possible?

If we can get the sales team members out of the highly reactive world of handling customer-support issues, they gain the ability to take more control of their time. That allows them to become proactive sellers. We want the whole team to be selling proactively, not reactively.

Going back to the story, the efforts to keep the planes in the air could not rest just on the support organization. The salespeople had a big role to play in this as well. They were going to have to trust the support organization to do their jobs. That seems kind of stupidly obvious, but there is a reason why it was not already happening.

Salespeople are fiercely defensive of their customer relationships, and it can be very difficult for many of them to trust someone else to impact those relationships. Given a choice, many salespeople will opt to take care of support issues for their customers themselves rather than trusting someone else to do it.

Time after time, when I've seen deep research done on time spent by salespeople, a huge amount of noncustomer-facing time was being spent by the salespeople personally taking care of customer-service issues. When we would talk to the salespeople about it, their reasoning was always the same:

> "I'm the only one who cares about my customer enough to be sure that this is taken care of."

While this is an admirable level of commitment to the customer, it's also a very self-centered view. In any well-run company, most people care about taking care of the customer. What this attitude is really indicative of is a lack of trust in the organization.

If you peel back the onion a bit when you detect this, you will inevitably hear horror stories about some incident in the past when organization X let down customer Y. What you rarely hear is anyone making a concerted effort to reach out to the leadership of organization X to fix the root causes of what went wrong in that customer story – they just choose to stay away from organization X instead.

Waldo Waldman's *Never Fly Solo* provides a great example of the type of thinking that we need to drive in our sales organizations to overcome this. Our salespeople need to feel like that are part of a larger organization that is dedicated to taking care of the customer. As sales leaders, it is our job to never condone the salesperson acting like a lone wolf when we see it, even when it seems justified by those horror stories.

Picture yourself in a sales meeting in which we have just heard a story about a problem at a customer site because customer service left them hanging on an order. The easy response for the sales manager is to commiserate and agree that those folks in customer service are idiots, that their leader is hard to work with, and that they are all out to get us.

The real sales leader's response is the hard one—get the full details, meet with the head of customer service, and work together to ensure that it never happens again.

Once the sales leaders have done this enough and set the tone of collaboration in the organization, the salespeople will start to do it themselves. They will start to reach out across the organization to fix the problem, not to assign blame. Don't kid yourself; this will not happen overnight. A transformation like that is going to take time and effort on your part, and there are going to be circumstances in which you are surely going to have to bite your tongue, but it's critical that you set this example for the sake of your team.

Why is this such an important topic? It's the single most effective way to get the most out of your sales team.

As with the Southwest Airlines story, the more time that we can get our salespeople in front of customers, the more revenue they are going to generate. It's kind of a simple equation. Getting more selling time out of your existing sales force is the simplest way to effectively get more feet on the street.

This is never going to be completely pure. No matter how efficient you are, a certain amount of back-office activity by salespeople is always necessary. Sales calls have to be planned and followed up on, expense reports have to be filed, and so on. The most effective sales forces absolutely minimize that time.

You may actually know your numbers, but if you don't, I've found that typically about 25 percent of a salesperson's time is spent with customers. Just do the math. If you can just get that to 50 percent, you will have effectively doubled the size of your sales force.

Rather than hiring more salespeople, most companies would benefit far more in investing in back-office resources or systems to get their salespeople back in front of their customers. The number-one objective of the sales-support teams and back office needs to be to "keep the planes in the air" and get the salespeople with customers in a selling mode.

This is hardly a revolutionary concept, but for something that businesses are widely in agreement on, the actions don't match the words. When budgets are tight, those back-office resources are often the first things to go—and they rarely come back later.

This is a bit like the elimination of bridge maintenance by municipal governments when budgets get tight. Nobody ever complains about it until the bridge falls down. The irony is that it can take years for that to happen—well after the people who made the decision to cut the maintenance are gone. They got a win that made them look good in the short term, but it hurt everyone in the long term. It ends up costing far more to replace the fallen bridge than the maintenance ever would have.

It's the same with any sales team, particularly if your offer has a longer sales cycle. The nonselling activities take the salespeople away from the missionary work that they should be doing for deals that won't close for a long time. The managers who make their budgets in the short term by having salespeople do those nonselling activities are often long gone by the time the price is really paid. It's the manager who comes along later who ends up paying the price—with a reduced pipeline of deals to work with to make the numbers.

To illustrate this, let's start with a list of tasks that are typical in most sales organizations:

* Sales-plan building
* Account planning and strategy
* Lead generation
* Lead qualification
* Customer research
* Value-proposition design
* Presentation design and preparation

* Sample procurement
* First customer sales call
* Mapping the politics of a deal
* Sales-call planning
* Sales calls (solo and joint)
* Sales-call follow-up
* Relationship-building events
* Trade shows
* Proposal generation
* Pricing strategy and approval
* Terms-and-conditions approval
* Customer negotiation
* Deal closing
* Order entry
* Project management (design approvals, change orders, delivery coordination)
* Resolving customer-service issues
* Smoothing over customer issues
* Long-term price-agreement maintenance
* Troubleshooting product issues
* Field-service support
* Channel-partner coordination
* Channel-partner planning
* Channel-partner training
* Customer training
* Team meetings
* Company meetings
* Manager reporting
* Product training
* Corporate-systems training
* Soft-skills training
* Expenses
* E-mail
* Dealing with internal IT systems

This is by no means meant to be an exhaustive list, but it does serve to illustrate the sheer scope of tasks that are loaded onto the salesperson. Another way to look at this list is to break it into a set of categories based on how much the salesperson should be involved in them.

<u>Things that the salesperson has to do:</u>

* First customer sales call
* Mapping the politics of a deal
* Sales-call planning
* Sales calls (solo and joint)
* Sales call follow-up
* Relationship-building events
* Trade shows
* Customer negotiation
* Deal closing
* Channel-partner coordination
* Channel-partner planning
* Smoothing over customer issues

These tasks are primarily customer facing and are best done by a salesperson. The salesperson should love doing all of them. The one caveat here would be the channel-partner tasks. Many organizations have specialized sales teams that are focused just on the channel, and in those cases, they should take on those tasks.

<u>Things that the salesperson should do but should be streamlined:</u>

* Team meetings
* Company meetings
* Manager reporting
* Product training
* Corporate-systems training

* Soft-skills training
* Expenses
* E-mail

Any of us—not just the salespeople—would love to eliminate this list from our world. Almost all of them fall into the category of "necessary evils." This raises an interesting question. Why is that? Why do we hate dealing with these basic things? Normally, it is because they are simply painful to get through or get done. The sales managers can do a lot to change that by how they lead their teams.

They should make their meetings short, engaging, and meaningful. They should only request reporting that is necessary and be sure as heck that they take the time to read, understand, and react to any reporting that they ask their team for. They should only have their team take training that is on point and make sure that the training is delivered well. They should have the simplest possible system for filing expenses—one that uses smartphone apps and automatic downloading from your credit-card vendor.

As far as e-mail goes, minimize it. Sales is a people business. If an e-mail is going to be more than one quick round of short exchanges, everyone should get the message to pick up the phone and call. Salespeople should be discouraged from copying the universe on every e-mail, and their managers need to lead by example themselves.

None of these items are going to go away, but smart sales managers can make them a lot less painful.

<u>Things that the salesperson should do with substantial help from others:</u>

* Sales-plan building
* Account planning and strategy

* Customer research
* Proposal generation
* Pricing strategy and approval
* Terms-and-conditions approval
* Long-term price-agreement maintenance

Sales-plan building and account planning are pretty critical activities for salespeople to be directly involved in. They need to feel that they have had a voice in determining the strategy and direction of both.

That being said, there is a lot that the finance and marketing departments can do to save time for the salespeople by providing them with reporting and tools that make it easy to research accounts, see sales histories, build plans toward quota, and lay out account plans. Marketing should have a library of account strategies for the salespeople to draw upon in their planning. The sales manager can also help immensely here by providing meaningful coaching to the salespeople through all of their planning.

Customer research should always be used by salespeople to plan their approaches to the customers, but they should not have to scramble for the information. Investing in a subscription to D&B or Hoovers can save a significant amount of time and ensure that real data is being used to make decisions.

Proposal generation, pricing strategy, T&C approvals and long-term price agreements should be led by the salesperson and discussed and strategized with the sales manager. These are some of the most important and meaningful coaching conversations that the manager can have, and there is real impact on both the hit rates of the deals involved as well as long-term profitability.

However, as important as these tasks are, poorly designed systems and processes in many companies often add an inordinate amount of work on the part of the salesperson to get them done.

If you are not already intimate with the processes involved in your company, act as a fly on the wall with one of your salespeople while he or she works to get a sense of it. This will tell you just how much of a burden it is on the salesperson and where you might be able to add some value by helping the business to simplify it.

Things that the salesperson should not be doing:

* Lead generation
* Lead qualification
* Presentation design and preparation
* Value-proposition design
* Troubleshooting product issues
* Field-service support
* Order entry
* Project management (design approvals, change orders, delivery coordination)
* Resolving customer-service issues
* Sample procurement
* Dealing with internal IT systems
* Channel-partner training
* Customer training

All of these are things that salespeople can and often do, but how smart is it to have then do them? Just because the salesperson *can* do them does not mean that this person *should* do them. Other members of the organization are going to be better at it and more effective. Everyone has to think in terms of the opportunity cost of having the salesperson do these things versus having less expensive resources do them.

Please don't take that "less expensive" comment too lightly. While salespeople are often more highly compensated than back office resources, that's not really what I am talking about in terms of the expense here. The real expense is the hidden opportunity cost that you pay by having that salesperson doing something other than the revenue generating tasks that only they are positioned to perform.

We will discuss a process for lead generation and lead qualification in much more detail in chapter 2-4. For now, suffice it to say that the generation and nurturing of leads should be done by teams optimized for the task. Doing this right is a very specialized process. Leads should not go to the salesperson until they have been nurtured to the point where there is desire on the part of the customer to speak with someone.

Presentation and value-proposition design should belong to marketing and/or product management depending on how you are structured. Salespeople should always be able to customize value propositions or presentations to match customers' particular circumstances, but they should be able to do this by drawing from a library of high-quality value propositions and presentations that have been designed by marketing and product-management professionals that are far more skilled at it.

As a side note, if you are trying to drive a higher level of collaboration between sales and marketing, the creation of this high-quality library should be at the top of your priority list. When the sales team members feel like they can go to the library and get material that they can really use in their sales calls, they will see real value and act accordingly when they interact with the marketing teams. The marketing and product-management teams will also get value as salespeople become more willing to invest their time and customer relationships to help them as they develop future content.

Troubleshooting and service are always best in the hands of true professionals, but salespeople often act as the first line of defense in some cases with a misplaced belief that this is the best way to ensure that their customers are taken care of. The only way to stop this is to have firm policies in place about it.

Sales management has to make this clear. If this is going on a lot, it could be indicating that there are some real, underlying customer-service issues. Over the long term, this is never fixed until the salespeople genuinely trust the services team—and vice versa.

Order entry, project management, customer service, and sample-procurement issues are also best left in the hands of focused professionals who deal daily in the minutiae, systems, and tasks involved. They will certainly need to interact frequently with the salesperson, but they should be the ones driving the process.

These teams need to be able to get things done in a timely enough fashion that the salesperson does not feel like it is necessary to take over to get things done in the customer's timeframe. We can't overlook the fact that these folks are at a desk and are reachable all day. This is a big factor in keeping things on schedule. When salespeople are required to manage these details, valuable time is often lost as they try to fit it in between sales calls or deal with things remotely.

It's probably a dream that salespeople—or any of us, for that matter—would not have to deal with the headaches of keeping our IT systems working. It's a reality that everyone has to face in the real world of the twenty-first century. The real question to ask ourselves in this regard is if we are being penny-wise and pound-foolish with the technology that we give our salespeople. Since the salespeople often work remotely and depend utterly on electronic links to keep things going, companies should invest in the highest-quality electronics for their teams that require the minimum amount of babysitting from IT.

Training is not quite as black-and-white as other issues. While training is best delivered by dedicated trainers, there are times when we use training as part of the sales process. A "lunch-and-learn" session introducing a new product can be a Trojan horse for a salesperson to get to meet customer team members whom they would not normally encounter—and they get to do so while they are demonstrating some real expertise. I've always been an advocate of this approach, but it is a slippery slope that can go well beyond selling if managers are not careful about what it is being used for.

Finally, for all of these issues, we should discuss the technique of the warm handoff. For every one of these tasks, even after they have been assigned to other parts of the organization, salespeople are still going to be called for help by the customer at some point in time. The trick here is in how they choose to handle these issues. They don't want to tell the customers, "That's not my job." But they also don't want to fall into the trap of just taking care of the issues, as that sets up expectations for the future.

The best way to handle these situations is to drive a warm handoff, like this:

> "You know, Bill, I'm not sure of the exact delivery date on that project. My project manager, Steve, is the one in the middle of those details. Let me get him on the phone with us. Steve? I've got Bill on the phone, and he needs to know the delivery date on project XYZ."

Trust me, once they have done that one or two times, Bill will understand that Steve is the right guy to deal with and will call him directly for those issues and will only call the salesperson when there is a problem that he or she really needs to be involved with.

At the end of the day, there is an entire community in any company that takes care of the customer. The salesperson is just the point person. All of the people in that community have to have a common mission of taking care of the customer and facilitating open, honest, and continuous communication between them. If all team members focus on their parts of the job and trusts the rest or the team to do theirs, everyone wins—especially the customer.

KEY TAKEAWAYS:

* Any activities that take away from selling time for the salesperson have a direct impact on the salesperson's productivity.
* Investing in sales-support resources can yield more sales productivity for the money than simply adding more salespeople.
* Salespeople have to trust the organization to take care of the nonselling tasks.

Chapter 1-7

Giving the Sales Team Focus

My friend Harvey Dunham has a great saying: "You can do any one thing, but you can't do everything." Salespeople, particularly ones who are struggling to make their numbers, can see opportunities everywhere. Harvey always knew how critical it is to help them narrow that view.

> It's January and time for annual planning meetings. Leadership wants to be anywhere *but* on the East Coast, so multiple teams set themselves up to do their meetings in Reno. It was a good setup, with plenary sessions in the morning to set the day, working sessions with each team to hammer out details, and then social time in the evenings to team build and trade ideas.
>
> There may also have been some drinking and gambling involved, but those could just be rumors.
>
> My team had spent three days working on growth plans and had an idea for a specific market that we had gotten very excited about. You know how groupthink can get a room going sometimes? We had that in spades. By the time we came out of the room, we were pretty sure that this idea was going to cure cancer. We were just going to need some resources from marketing to put together the tools for us.

As soon as the social hour got going, I searched out Tom, the head of marketing. I made sure that he had a drink and proceeded to give him my very best pitch on our cure for cancer. I was passionate. I was glib. I'm sure that I was compelling, and I am reasonably sure that there was no spinach in between my teeth. Despite all of this, it was clear that this was going nowhere with Tom.

I was devastated. I could not believe that Tom was not budging on this. Sure, it was not directly aligned with the overall strategy, but this was going to make a huge difference for the few of us handling that specialized market.

The irony is that as passionate as I was about that idea, for the life of me, I cannot remember what it was or what it was going to do for us. What I do remember—and will never forget—was Tom's response that just shut me down when I pressed him for why he was not willing to deviate from his main strategy. He looked me straight in the eye and said:

"Where we focus, we win."

I'd like to say that I instantly saw the genius of his statement and got my team to go along immediately, but that's not quite the case. I was pretty ticked at him in the moment, and it's possible that I might have said a bad word or two under my breath at the time. But later, when I learned to take a wider view of the world, I came to saw the genius of that statement, particularly for a sales team.

Tom was actually quoting Harvey Dunham at the time. That saying was a mantra that Harvey ended virtually every presentation that he gave to his sales team with. Years later, when I got the opportunity to lead that same team, I did it as well.

A sales team is faced with all kinds of potential directions in which to go, and distractions come up every time that a phone rings and they see an opportunity for new business. Salespeople can be a bit like that dog in the movie *Up*, stopping every other thought the moment he thinks that he sees a squirrel.

The only way that a sales team can defend against that is to have a sustained focus on their targeted customers. They have to be able to manage distractions so that they minimize reactive selling time and follow a proactive-selling philosophy.

This takes me to a fundamental rule that I have come to realize:

> **The real difference in the success of a salesperson is their relative ratio of proactive versus reactive activity.**

It's the sales manager's job to help the salesperson get to the right ratio through the coaching that they give, the systems that they put around the person, and the work that they do with the organization, as we discussed in the previous chapter.

We will talk a lot more about how to best help a sales team execute proactively around the pipeline in chapter 3, but the principles of what I call "proactive selling" are pretty basic:

<u>Plan</u>
The salesperson plans everything both to handle more things and to do them more effectively. This is the very definition of being proactive. The best salespeople are planners, and when they make those plans, they don't put them in drawers. They follow them and constantly modify them to match the evolving state of affairs.

<u>Prepare</u>
The salesperson prepares for every encounter with customers, thinking through all of the likely questions and concerns. The best salespeople never "wing it" in sales calls. They over prepare for every encounter with their customers.

<u>Execute</u>
The salesperson executes around all the core disciplines, always following a consistent process. The sales organization should have

a process for account planning, lead management, sales-call planning, and pipeline management. The best salespeople execute around those processes with rigor and discipline to ensure that no balls are dropped.

Follow Up

The salesperson follows up on every commitment. Whether a commitment is made to a prospect, customer, or channel partner, every time a task is committed to in a meeting or on a phone call, the customer looks at it as a promise. The best salespeople are on top of all of these to drive business forward and earn trust.

The processes that sales leadership establishes will determine the degree to which their salespeople can become proactive.

For all of the proactive-planning elements that we will discuss in different parts of this book, there will be pushback from the salespeople around the concept of writing them into the CRM. Common refrains will be, "I know all of those things and have it all planned out in my head" or "I've been doing this for twenty years; I don't have to do such basic planning."

I need to be clear on this point as it has been central to so many debates that I have had on getting data into a CRM. The real reason for salespeople to write this stuff down is not for the sales manager to see in a report—it is for *them*. The simple act of writing something down, of having to refine the thought into one or two concise sentences, forces clarity of thought on the part of the person doing it.

The salesperson may well have a general idea of what the objective of a sales call is, but once he or she has to say it in one sentence, it is that much clearer. The objective will be that much less likely to fall to the wayside when the inevitable distractions come during the sales call.

There is one huge caveat here. As adamant as I am about the value of putting things that drive the sales process into the CRM, that's also where I draw the line. Far too many CRMs have become overly complicated by organizations trying to do too many things with them—and requiring salespeople to put information into the tool that adds no value to the process of selling.

There is a much better chance of a sales team truly adopting a CRM when salespeople can tell that what they are required to put into the tool actually drives their selling activities.

Finally, no matter how complex the overall sales strategy may be, sales managers need to give their teams a set of rules or guidelines that illustrate the philosophy that they want team members to follow.

The more complex the strategy, the more important this is, as it anchors the team to a core concept.

Any manager is going to want to design these guidelines to match both their own style and the mission that they are trying to set. As an example, these are the rules that have worked best for me in the past. With the teams that I have led, I would just present the rules themselves, but I have included some more detailed explanations with each to be sure that the story of each rule can be understood.

1. **When in doubt, take care of the customer.**
   Yes, this can seem just a tad obvious, but it gives permission for the salesperson to know that the manager will give air cover in the event that he or she has to make a time-critical decision. This does not mean that someone should go rogue and not work with the rest of the team; it means that everyone should make it the first priority to ensure that the customer is always cared for.

2. **Never walk away from an order.**

   We do far too much work to get to the point where we might have a customer give us an order to let go of the opportunity lightly. The team members need to know that when they have deals that might go off the table, they should elevate issues or internal barriers to management so that a decision can be made together on what to do. Far too many times, I have seen salespeople walk away from orders because they just assumed that the organization could not or would not agree to something when the organization would actually have been happy to do so.

3. **Don't sell it until you can drop it on your foot!**

   Many of the people who have worked for me in the past still refer to this as "Forsgard's Law." As much as we want to and need to trust the organization to deliver new products on a schedule, the reality is that inventing new products is not a predictable process. I don't know about you, but I have almost never seen a product launch on its original schedule.

   How you define this depends on the history in your particular organization. In some places, the track record six months out is excellent and can be the guideline. In other places, history shows that selling the product before it is actually in the warehouse is a risk.

   There can always be times when exceptions are made to the rule. Even though it's my rule, I've made a few myself. Just be sure that exceptions are only made after much consideration and deliberation on the risks and rewards and that the entire team (the salesperson, sales management, product management, and engineering) is involved in the decision to make the exception.

Nothing will poison a long-term customer relationship more than leaving the customer hanging on the promise of a new product or solution.

4. **Think "Yes, if..." *not* "No, because..."**

   This can be a bit of a psychological game, but you need to have your team members always thinking in terms of how they could solve a problem, not why it can never be solved. This is especially pertinent in negotiations with customers—when they throw something at your salespeople, you want them to think about the ways that they can safely say yes and secure the order.

5. **Be responsive.**

   We may have already beaten this horse to death, but I can't emphasize enough how important this is for a sales organization. This is a price of entry with any customer, yet it too often falls to the wayside when the distractions come. This also ties to how the salesperson communicates with "wingmen" in the organization. The wider team working on an account or a deal should never get blindsided by a situation. Most CRMs have excellent tools to keep the team updated; the salesperson and the rest of the organization just have to commit to using them.

6. **Elevate issues.**

   The sales team needs to know that griping about something doesn't get it fixed. If there is an issue, step one is to make sure that the right people know about it and are trying to deal with it. More often than not, this is your role as the sales manager. Your job is to navigate the organization and try to find the fixes to the issues that your salespeople bring to you—hopefully along with a "Yes, if" solution.

7. **Don't let knowledge get stale.**

   In today's world, customers have access to far more information about products and solutions than they did in the past. They don't need the salesperson to walk them through a brochure; they can read that on the web. Study after study has shown that customers have over two-thirds of the information that they need by the time that they are talking to a salesperson. What they need from a salesperson is expertise and insight. To be able to have that, the modern salesperson has to be in a perpetual state of learning and not just relying on periodic training classes. Always be learning. Always be teaching.

8. **Be a part of the wider organization.**

   As we have already discussed, the sales team cannot exist in a vacuum. Any part of the organization that touches or supports the customer is part of the sales team and needs to feel that way. Particularly since salespeople are normally deployed away from headquarters and operations, they need to work hard to stay engaged with the entire organization (including adjacent sales organizations).

9. **Do things on time.**

   As much as we have emphasized responsiveness to customers, we need to be equally responsive inside the organization. The team members need to know that you expect them to act like professionals and have all of the basics covered. CRM work, expenses, and all of the back-office parts of their jobs should be done on time without anyone having to be chased.

10. **Never, never, call me Charlie.**

    Unless your name is also Charles and you are particularly pedantic about it, this one might not matter as much to the success of your sales force, but it always worked for me.

KEY TAKEAWAYS:

* The real difference in the success of salespeople is their relative ratio of proactive versus reactive activity.
* Proactive selling revolves around planning, preparing, executing, and following up.
* You can give your team focus on their mission by establishing a clear set of guidelines on how you want them to operate.

Chapter 2

Place

As I came up as a young salesman, I thought a lot about what I was selling, how I was selling it, and to whom I was selling it. I never gave much thought to *where* I was selling. I was simply hired and assigned to sell a set of products to a set of accounts in a territory and trained on what to sell them. It took getting embarrassed by my CEO to make me really think about that.

> I was running a small business unit in the company. The job was very meaningful to me as it included a product line that I had spent quite a bit of my career selling and it had a dedicated sales force that I had a large part in building.
>
> Once a quarter, I went to headquarters to present a business review to the CEO and his senior staff. The CEO was young and full of energy. He had come up through the company ranks and at one time had run the central manufacturing plant for the products that I was responsible for. He was a real thinker.
>
> You had to be nimble on your feet during these reviews as he was almost always going to come up with a question that you were not going to have thought of and prepared an answer for.

In one particular review, we had just gone over the current sales team deployment for the central product line—the sales team that I had helped to build. At the time, the United States was split into thirty-two sales areas, with managers who were accountable for the sales of all of the company's core products. The specialized sales team for my product line was made up of forty salespeople, with at least one of them deployed in each of the thirty-two sales areas.

A slide with the map showing this deployment had been up on the screen, and I had just blipped past it to get to my next slide when he stopped me and asked me to go back.

"Why do you have a specialist in each of the sales areas?"

It was a simple question, but those are the ones that usually get you in the most trouble.

"We've found that dedicating a specialist to each area is the best way to get support from the area managers and drive the rest of their team to help sell the specialized products."

"Why?"

"Well, that gives us force multiplier of just a bit of all those salespeople's time and attention. It nets us more feet on the street, getting us to more customers."

"Let me ask you this another way. Pretend that this is your own business and that you had the budget to hire forty salespeople from scratch. Is this where you would put them?"

This one really hit me between the eyes. I actually took a very long pause to think about the answer.

"No. I would not put them there at all."

"Where would you put them?"

"I'd put them in the markets with the most potential business for the salespeople to target. For the smaller markets, it's going to take a long time to build the business to the point where the salespeople would really pay for themselves."

"Then why haven't you already done that?"

Talk about feeling stupid. I'm sitting there with a sales deployment that is costing the company over $4 million a year, and it's laid out based on historical practice and a "peanut buttering" of resources to ensure that every area manager is happy that he or she has a specialist to lean on.

That was not a strategy for sales growth. It was a strategy for political happiness in the organization.

I always like to say that the most important lessons we learn come from our most embarrassing mistakes, and this is certainly one of mine. It taught me that you can't just let historical inertia drive the deployment of a sales team—the market and the opportunities in it have to be the real drivers of it.

(It also taught me the value of the kind of coaching questions that we talk about so much in this book. That CEO was a master of them.)

In this section, we will look closely at how to ensure that you are sending your salespeople to the right places. We will start with looking at the geographic mapping of the opportunities and then move on to how to align your salespeople with the right accounts. We will look at how to perform account planning that actually gets used, give the right leads to the right people, make sure that we plan and execute sales calls better, and engage fully with channel partners.

Chapter 2-1

Go Where the Money Is

After that meeting, I thought a lot about how to explain the concept of not just spreading salespeople around, and then I remembered this great story.

> Willie Sutton was a famous bank robber who stole over $2 million during his career. He was known for daring robberies in which he often used disguises, earning him a notorious reputation.
>
> As the story goes, after Willie was captured by the New York City police, a crowd of reporters surrounded him and one of them shouted, "Willie, why do you rob banks?"
>
> Willie replied, *"Because that's where the money is!"*

Alas, like many great stories, this one is apocryphal. Willie himself denied ever saying it and blamed it on a reporter who just wanted to fill out some copy. However, it does illustrate a key point for deploying a sales team—you go where the money is.

That simple rule is also easy to misinterpret. As in the story in the introduction to this chapter, most sales teams get laid out according to where the existing or previous business was. While it is important to maintain that business, it does not necessarily relate to where the potential business for the future is.

Let me give you a simple example. The map below is a plot of a particular type of customers in North America. It has a very small dot for each one of about 95,000 customers.

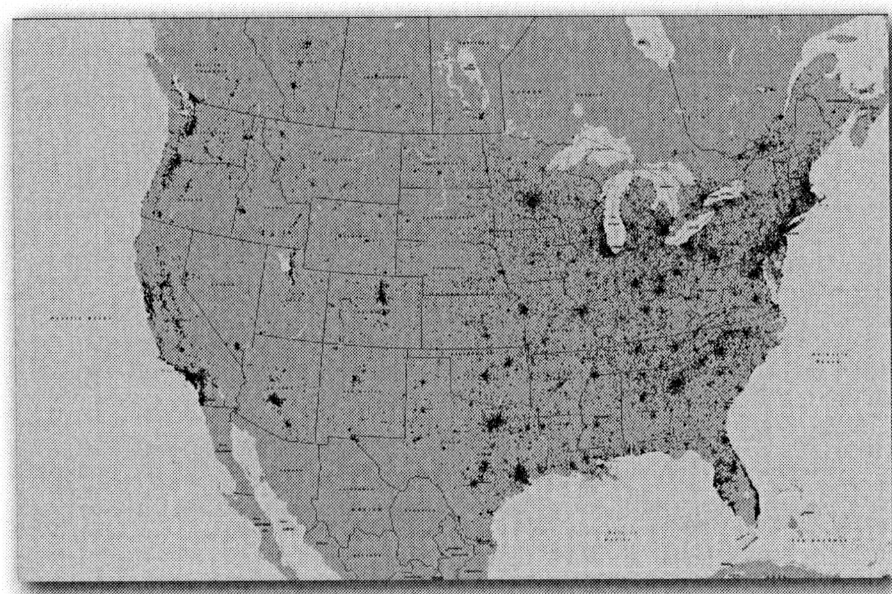

(Figure 2.1.1)

What is most interesting about this chart is that the type of customer is almost immaterial. I've seen similar plots of all kinds of customer types, and they all end up looking about the same. With very few exceptions, most types of customers are still going to align with general population density, as this map does.

Depending on what you are selling, the exceptions can matter. Certain niche products and markets, such as ones tied to natural-resource extraction, are going to end up requiring salespeople who are where those natural resources are, not the population.

The point is to understand the target customers for your product and map them so that you can see where the business opportunity is. If you are going to execute a growth strategy, you want to position your salespeople in the most target-rich environments possible.

To do this right, you need three maps.

1. The first map lays out your existing sales team. Depending on the complexity of your sales force, you may want to show a variety of details:

    * Locations of sales people
    * Sales-region boundaries
    * Locations of managers
    * Locations of applications engineers
    * Locations of support staff
    * Locations of channel partners
    * Boundaries of channel partners' authorized markets
    * Locations of rep firms
    * Boundaries of rep firms' authorized markets
    * Locations of manufacturing plants
    * Locations of distribution centers

    Ideally, this map should be set up to use as an overlay on top of the other two map types.

2. The second map lays out your existing customer base. I've found that this can best be done either as a series of dots for each customer location or with objects that vary with size relative to the revenue of each customer. How useful either is visually comes down to the number of customers and the scale that you are looking at. If you have a significant customer base, simple dots tend to work best.
3. The final map lays out your potential customer base. Using SIC codes and a database from sources like Hoovers, you can establish lists of

customers that best fit your target-customer types and then plot them on a map just like the one above.

When you overlay the first map on top of the other two, you are going to see just how well your sales force aligns with both your existing and potential customers.

The first thing that you want to look for are the gaps:

* Are there locations where there are significant densities of existing customers but no salespeople?
* Are there locations where there are significant densities of potential customers but few existing ones?
* Do your channel partners align with where the existing and potential customers are?

Next, you want to look where you might be overloaded:

* In equivalently dense markets, do you have the same numbers of salespeople?
* In equivalently dense markets, do you have the same amount of channel coverage?

A lot of this is going to come more from art rather than science, and you are going to need to get a feel for what kind of coverage densities make the most sense for your business. One good rule of thumb can be to pick your best-performing markets and use the densities of salespeople and channel partners there as guidelines for other markets.

The temptation that you will have to fight is to "peanut butter" your resources around your entire coverage area, like I did in my story.

That can lead to some tough decisions. You might have a great salesperson sitting in Bozeman, Montana. Are you better off with that salesperson sitting in a tiny market or putting a resource in the Northeast Corridor? There certainly might be some customers in Bozeman, but there are a lot more of them in the Northeast.

The other thing to watch out for is how much you allow your team to specialize. If you get too refined here, you can end up with a lot of salespeople passing each other on the highway or, worse yet, in the air. There are certainly offers that are so specialized as to require some of this. Just be aware of it as you lay out your coverage model.

The trick here is not to become a prisoner of how things have been done in the past. Lay out the data, and then ask the questions as objectively as possible—pretend that you are starting with a clean sheet of paper.

If you were to lay out channel partners and salespeople from scratch, where would you put them? In what order of priority? This has to be your starting point.

Be like Willie Sutton—go where the money is.

KEY TAKEAWAYS:

* Historical deployment of salespeople can be a dangerous habit.
* Put your salespeople where the existing business is and where you have the highest density of potential customers to grow with.

Chapter 2-2

Matching Your Accounts to Your Salespeople.

Once you figure out the geographical territories in which to put your salespeople, the next step is to look at exactly to which accounts in that territory they should be assigned. The thought process for this should be as much about the salesperson as it is about the account.

> I'm meeting in a hotel room on Nanjing Road in Shanghai with one of my salesmen. Bill and I are huddled around an iPhone on the desk in the room, using the speakerphone to talk to our team in the United States.
>
> Six months ago, Bill had come to my strategic-accounts team as a business-development manager. His role was going to be to add new strategic accounts to our portfolio, and I had sent him after a set of accounts that fit our main offering.
>
> As a primary focus, I had given Bill one high-value target. The account was known for being very price sensitive, and my expectations were low; it was a long shot and would probably take years to pay off.
>
> Bill spent several months diligently penetrating the account, working his way from contact to contact to see what they needed and to let

them know what we could do. It was the kind of rock-solid missionary work that has to be done to penetrate a large account but that very few salespeople have the skill and patience to do.

At one of their key plants, the customers had been working with a major competitor for some time, and they were fairly entrenched. We all know that every now and then, companies stumble, and that is just what happened here. Suddenly there was an opening, and Bill had already taken meetings with several of the key stakeholders for the decision to switch the business over.

Bill quickly reconnected with all of the stakeholders and started to rough out the type of proposal that we would have to make to win the business. In the space of a month, he met with them in the United States, Europe, and China and was now back in China again to continue the fight.

Due to Bill's work, we knew what it was going to take to get the business, and now we had to convince our company that it was worth the risk to take it away from our entrenched competitor. We had laid out our case as best we knew how, and finally that night, huddled around that little iPhone, we got the permission to move forward.

Bill ran with it and had an MOU in place in a matter of weeks. Over the course of the coming months, he got the business flowing. That's when we ran into a big dilemma.

What had to be done now at the account was a *lot* of detail management—not just managing the transition of the business, but also getting the full contract finalized and signed.

If Bill dove into all of that, he was not going to be able continue the rest of the business-development work that he had underway. I

> brought in a strategic-account manager to lead the startup of the business and free Bill up to do what he did best—land new accounts.
>
> That's where we ran into a new problem. Bill did not want to let the account go. In a very real sense, this was his "baby," and he wanted to see it all the way through.
>
> Bill understood the reasoning of why his skills were better suited to business development, but that did not take away the emotional response to having to move away from this thing that he had created. Even though Bill always got the credit for landing the business, things stayed tense between him and the salesperson who took over the account for some time to come.

The problem that Bill had here was that in his heart of hearts, he was a hunter. The work that he enjoyed doing—and was very skilled at—was sizing up potential accounts and then penetrating them strategically. The work that needed to be done at the account was not hunter work; it was farmer work. Although Bill understood that and had been paid handsomely and recognized for landing the account, he had come to think of this eight-figure account as his.

As I have said before, this is not to say that hunters are more valuable than farmers. What they are is different. Each requires a different personality and skill set to really perform well. It's not necessarily a binary choice. I've worked with plenty of salespeople who were hybrids, but even they tended to lean more one way than the other.

By no means was Bill the only case that I had ever seen of this; it was just one of the most extreme. It happens in companies all the time and has frustrated sales leaders forever. You take someone who is highly skilled at hunting. The person succeeds and bags the huge account, and then he or she is so buried with handling the details of that account that the person never has the bandwidth to get back out and bag another one.

Usually, the salesperson is also miserable, even if he or she won't admit that the reason why is a hatred of all that farming work.

This gets to the root of the problem that we want to discuss in this chapter—how do you ensure that you are assigning your salespeople to the accounts that best align with their skill sets? Part of this is knowing how to classify your salespeople, and part of it is knowing how to classify your accounts.

From chapters 1-1 through 1-3, we discussed extensively how to evaluate your salespeople. Although there is a lot of nuance to classifying our salespeople, for the purposes of this chapter, we will use just the categories of hunters, farmers, and hybrids.

LaVon Kerner at Revenue Storm has a very clear way of laying out these categories for deployment.

> **A pure account leader** (Hunter) A professional tasked to win high risk opportunities (i.e. competitively held, previously lost, adverse environment) or to accelerate the acquisition of new markets, new account divisions, new geographies, new accounts.
>
> > Attributes: Assertive, confident, high risk tolerance. Needs recognition. Unrelenting, persistent, single-minded focus, independent, competitive, impatient, need for variety.
>
> **A pure account manager** (Farmer) A professional tasked to cultivate, grow and protect revenue in existing accounts while achieving high customer satisfaction and valued relationships.
>
> > Attributes: Relational. Risk intolerant, prefers known environment, collaborative, predictable and dependent.
>
> **A hybrid** (Hunting-Farmer) A professional tasked with both protecting while significantly expanding an existing account's

wallet-share by penetrating new areas (i.e. Divisions, geographies, and subsidiaries).

Once you have your salespeople classified, you need to think about how to classify your accounts, and the classification of accounts can be a slippery slope. You can get into industries, applications, company size, and a long list of other attributes.

Depending how you are going to market, you may still need to have some process around this, but for the purposes of helping a salesperson focus on the right accounts, I've found that this works better with a functional breakdown. This functional classification will drive the type of activity that you will do with the account as well as the time horizon that you are going to do it in.

In our process, we classify these accounts as either conversion, extraction, or retention.

Conversion

Conversion accounts are accounts that are currently buying from your competition. This is the classic "new account" and has the longest selling cycle.

Extraction

Extraction accounts are currently buying from you, but you have a small percentage of their overall spend with the bulk of their business still being done with your competition. This is a shorter selling cycle as there are already established relationships in place.

Retention

Retention accounts are existing customers in which you are getting about as high a percentage of their existing business as you can reasonably expect. Your main mission with these accounts is simply not to lose any ground with them.

One of the beauties of this classification system is that it is functional, so you take a lot of the interpretation out of it. There is not a lot of interpretation in how much of a customer's wallet is being spent on you. Once you have this classification and the classification of your salespeople done, you can decide the model that you want to use to map them to each other.

Precisely how you do this is going to depend on the size of your sales team.

If you have a large sales team, it may make sense to dedicate a team of hunters to go after conversion accounts, particularly if you are intending to target large strategic accounts that are going to take some time to penetrate. The rest of your team will be made up of farmers and hybrids who will get the most business possible out of your extraction and retention accounts.

If you have a more moderately sized sales team, you may not be able to afford the luxury of dedicated hunters. This will require more of a hybrid approach with a balance between all of the account types. Hunters should have account packages that skew more heavily to conversion accounts. Farmers should have account packages that skew more heavily to retention and extraction accounts. Hybrids become very valuable in smaller sales forces as you can use them with any of these account packages.

As you start to plan around these deployments, be sure to keep timing in mind. Regardless of the sales cycle of your product, conversion business will always take substantially longer to develop than extraction or retention. Regardless of the size of your sales team, you need to have enough extraction and retention accounts to deliver short-term growth while working their conversion accounts for the long term.

In the case of individual salesperson, how you measure and incentivize him or her also has to consider the salesperson's mix of classified accounts. Conventional quotas work well with salespeople who have all retention and extraction accounts. Salespeople with more conversion accounts need to have longer-term measurements. If your sales team ends up with a mix of all three types, you need to balance the assignments so that they have enough extraction and retention accounts to meet short-term objectives while working enough conversion accounts to build for the future. It's all about understanding this well enough to balance it out.

When we talk about balance here, we really have to mean it. Because conversion-account activity is not for the short term, it is easy to kick it down the road when more immediate demands come up from the extraction and retention accounts. Don't let that happen. At a minimum, you should require a certain number of sales calls on conversion accounts every month to prevent this.

In my experience, it is hard for an outside salesperson to properly manage more than about twenty-five accounts. (That's just an average; depending on the size of the accounts and the geography, this can go lower or higher.) With that as a starting point, a good balance would be fifteen retention and extraction accounts and about ten conversion accounts.

While the retention and extraction accounts should be relatively firm in their assignments for the year, the conversion accounts may change often as the discovery process uncovers information that changes the desirability of specific accounts. Just be sure to rotate in a new conversion target whenever you take one off the list.

That gives you the basic model of how to align your hunters, farmers, and hybrids against conversion, extraction, and retention accounts. Over time, you need to keep in mind that during the life of any account, it is naturally going to move between these classifications—and that can change how you will deploy your salespeople to them. This evolution will be easy to manage as long as you have decided on the model that you will use to map your salespeople and keep your classifications objective.

Just remember that classifying accounts is an ongoing process, not an event. In any sales organization, your account data and information are your crown jewels. Guard and manage that data accordingly.

As you implement the system, you are going to want to add in some additional information that is more specific to your business and markets.

On the salesperson side, beyond classifying hunters and farmers, you will also want to factor in specific product, application, or industry expertise that is needed for specific accounts. You will also want to factor in overall competency and experience versus the complexity or degree of difficulty of the accounts in question.

On the account side, you will want to look at the demographic data on each account. This is going to tell you as much as possible about their markets, industry, and applications.

I am a huge advocate of getting this data into the CRM itself and having it linked to the real world to stay current. This puts all of your planning and selection data in one place and give you "one source of truth" for the information. Your sales data should also be there to allow you to factor in size and opportunity.

What kind of information am I talking about?

<u>Account Demographics</u>

D-U-N-S Numbers

At the end of the day, maintaining an account database can be a nightmare. Between inconsistent naming conventions and people just trying to get information into the system quickly, you are inevitably going to end up with lots of duplicate accounts. The best solution that I have found is to use the Dun & Bradstreet

D-U-N-S numbers in each account. D&B provides just one D-U-N-S number per physical location, making it a fairly reliable tool for detecting duplicates.

SIC Codes

If you are subscribing to D&B, you can also purchase demographic information along with it, such as number of employees or revenue. These are certainly useful, but if you get nothing else, get the SIC code. At the end of the day when you are trying to assign accounts, one of the most important things to know is what the accounts really do.

One caution. While the database information for SIC codes is certainly valuable, it is not always accurate. It can be best to design your tool to allow the salespeople to override the SIC code if they know better. As the codes can be a bit confining sometimes, adding a field where the salesperson can put a plain English description can save you a lot of time later whenever you scrub the data. These verbatim descriptions are the best data that you can have. You can see an example of how to do this in chapter 2-3, in which account planning is discussed.

Finally, D&B is just an example of a system to use—there are plenty out there, and some are far better suited to different parts of the world. The point is to have some kind of objective system to give you a clean ID for your accounts and to help you pull in supplementary data.

Sales Data

Internal company ERP

While you can use the deals closed in your CRM itself as one measure of the volume with the account, there are multiple reasons why that can turn out to be inaccurate—particularly if your salespeople make a lot of multiyear deals.

Your company ERP system is normally the best source of truth for this, but most companies do not give salespeople access to this data, and when they do, they are rarely simple to interact with. Linking the data to the CRM system is often the best way to overcome this. As long as you either require account numbers to be input into the CRM or use D-U-N-S numbers in both systems, the linkage can be relatively straightforward to set up.

Channel-Partner Point-of-Sale Data

Most corporate ERP systems are set up to only keep track of sales data on direct accounts and channel partners as those are the entities transacting business with the company. For indirect accounts, that are served by your channel partners, the only source of this information is point-of-sale (POS) data from those channel partners.

Many companies require POS data in their channel-partner agreements, but few of them have been able to use the data effectively due to the challenges of scrubbing this data to the point where it can be accurately mapped to the right accounts.

There are a number of vendors that have figured out effective methodologies for this and will gather the information from your channel partners, scrub it, and map it into your ERP or CRM systems. If you need a starting point, a company called Zyme has been one of the best that I have seen.

It should also not be overlooked that getting this information into the CRM is one of the simplest ways for a company to get their salespeople to value their CRM. When the data is in the CRM, they can gain intelligence on their accounts from multiple sources in one place. This is yet another example of how we can have the CRM give something back to the salesperson.

As critical as working with this data is, getting it clean and keeping it clean can be a major headache. There are two big lessons that I have learned in many years of dealing with it:

First, working with this data is a process, not an event. Once you have figured out what you want to do and have driven the implementation, don't take the cheap approach. Appoint and empower a data steward to stay on top of this data, and perpetually scrub it to ensure that you have good data hygiene. The minute that the data starts to develop major issues, it is effectively useless—particularly if you are also using it in your sales-incentive process.

Secondly, although there are many services out there that promise to be able to accurately scrub this data with an AI or some kind or fuzzy logic, as of 2017, the state-of-the-art systems are still a long way from being effective. In my experience, running these systems can often result in your data being less accurate than when you started. A properly trained entry-level employee armed with a D&B account and Google can validate quite a few accounts every day. It can be very cost effective to set up a small team of these folks under your data steward to perpetually scrub the data—particularly the links to your ERP system.

Depending on the size of your company and how much you are able to invest, these data systems might be out of reach. Even if you are at a company able to invest in them, these data systems are going to take some time to get in place if you do not already have them.

Don't let any of that prevent you from using this methodology for your account classification and assignments. You can start just with conversion, extraction, and retention classifications from the local knowledge of your sales team to get started. That is enough to map the accounts to your salespeople and do a smarter deployment.

Over time, your data capabilities may grow and allow more sophistication, but the basic philosophy does not change.

The bottom line is that if you put some real logic and a balanced approach into how you are assigning accounts to your salespeople, you will be taking a huge step toward helping them to be more effective than they could be on their own.

You are giving them focus on the accounts that can best help them to make their numbers.

KEY TAKEAWAYS:

* It's easy to think that any salesperson can sell to any account, but every salesperson has attributes that make him or her better matches for specific accounts.
* The differences between salespeople do not make them better or worse—knowing that they are hunters, farmers, or hybrids just tells you the types of accounts that they will best engage with.
* Accounts break into three basic categories: conversion, extraction, and retention.
* Getting and maintaining a high level of data hygiene in your account data needs to be a continuous process.
* You will get the most productivity from your sales team when you align the characteristics of your salespeople with the account types with which they best align.

Chapter 2-3

Keeping Your Account Plans out of a Drawer

Almost every company out there does some level of account planning with its salespeople. Most of those sales plans get put into drawers as soon as they are written and are never looked at again.

Let's talk again about my friend Scott Day. Scott was an outstanding salesperson who came over to our company from a major competitor, bringing all of his customers with him—providing an important early lesson in the value of relationships.

A wiry marathon runner who cares a lot about people, Scott quickly took the younger salespeople under his wing and helped all of us to raise our games.

It was not long before he was promoted to manager. Shortly after he took over our team, he called us all in for a multiday meeting and kicked it off with his basics on account planning.

Prior to this, our attempts at account planning had been haphazard at best.

Every few years, someone at corporate would come up with a new format for account plans that we would be required to fill out and put into big binders that nobody ever read. Typically, the plans themselves were not so much plans as they were corporate analyses of the accounts with all kinds of demographic and financial data about the customers.

Scott had a much simpler approach that boiled down to just three things: strategy, tactics, and execution. To build a plan, you just had to answer three questions, all of which were to be answered in just a couple of sentences:

> What does this customer do?
>
> What is your overall strategy for approaching the account?
>
> What are the key three or four tactics that you need to execute in the coming year to support that strategy?

That was it.

He had us all line up our computers on the tables in the room and told us that we were not leaving until we had a plan ready for every one of our accounts. He would be right there with us to coach us on them, but the plans had to be done, or we were wasting our time in the field.

His point was that without account plans, we were just reacting to what happened there. With a plan, we would start to control the narratives at our accounts and actually make things happen instead.

We sat down at the tables with extension cords everywhere (this was long before they gave laptops to salespeople) and got to work. Aside from the time that I tripped over a cord and wiped out all of one of my fellow salesperson's work, it went well.

Then, Scott threw us the real curveball. He actually expected us to execute on these plans and scheduled updates with us every quarter to check progress on our goals. We were not going to write them just to toss them in a drawer and then keep simply reacting to whatever happened at the account.

The simplicity of this approach let us get down to the essence of what we wanted to do with each account. Since we had been conditioned for so long to come up with account plans that were mostly filler, it actually took some work to shift gears. With more coaching from Scott, it turned into an exciting project because we were talking about what we were going to do to grow instead of just plugging in data.

Even more powerful than the simplicity of these plans was the effectiveness of the process. Because we knew that he was going to follow up on the progress to the plans, we made sure that we were getting the tasks done all through the quarter—and the results started to show. Over the course of the next few years, we all started to beat our numbers consistently.

Many salespeople start to tune out the minute that managers start to talk about planning. In my experience, that has been because most of the planning exercises that they get pulled into are just for form and to check off some boxes, as opposed to actually bringing clarity to how they think about what they are doing to drive business in their accounts.

What I loved about this approach is that it boiled the planning down to its essence—understanding who you were dealing with, having a simple strategy to follow, and driving the execution around tactics that would enable that strategy.

This takes us to another place where we want the salesperson to "never fly solo" and engage the larger organization. We can make these account plans—and the planning process itself—even more powerful by integrating the programs and campaigns that have been developed by the marketing and product-management teams.

In an ideal world, the marketing and product-management teams create a library of strategies and related tactics for different customer types that salespeople can draw from while customizing them for each account. This gives you the benefit of engaging those resources while keeping the process simple.

The salespeople end up viewing the marketing and product-management teams as genuinely adding value as they see how the tools that they produce can directly apply to their accounts. The salesperson does not have to invent everything from scratch; he or she can draw from a library of ideas and then customize and enhance them.

You may want to put more into your sales plans than just this basic format. Just remember, as a rule, if any element of an account plan is not going to add direct value for the salesperson or give greater clarity of thought around the account, then it is superfluous.

Before we move on, I want to talk a bit more about strategy versus tactics. These concepts are often mixed up in people's heads, along with goals and objectives. I can't tell you how many times I have asked a salesperson to tell me his or her strategy and gotten back a list of goals or tactics that have been planned.

Let's start by segregating what we want to happen from how we are going to make it happen. Goals and objectives are things that we want to achieve. Strategy and tactics are the things that we do to meet those goals and objectives.

A strategy is an overall plan, while the tactics are the things that you do to execute that plan.

The best definition of strategy that I ever heard was that it is a filter that you can use to hold up in front of all of your tactics. If they don't fit that filter, then they don't belong there.

This can be hard to get across to people as a definition, but you can make it more concrete with real examples during coaching sessions with the salespeople while they are developing their plans. This is a great opportunity to use the same types of coaching questions that we have brought into play in several other parts of this book.

> What is the main outcome that you want to achieve with this customer?
>
> What is the overall approach that you will use to achieve that outcome?

That overall approach is your strategy.

> What are the measurable steps that you are going to meet to drive that overall approach?
>
> What are the actions that you are going to take to make those steps happen?

Those actions are your tactics.

Normally, the salesperson does have a strategy in mind subconsciously; he or she just has not been able to state it clearly. The problem is that since the salesperson can't state the strategy clearly, it can't really be used to filter out the tactics that don't support it and that are really distractions.

To help them filter out those distracting tactics, you can ask these questions:

> Why do you want to use that tactic?

What reaction at the customer do you intend to drive with that tactic?

How does that reaction help you to reach the main outcome that you want to achieve with the customer?

As you work though the answers to those questions for each tactic, a theme is bound to evolve, and you can help the salesperson to see the strategy that was tying their tactics together. They can then use it to filter out the noise.

This is an area where skillful coaching from the sales manager can really help the salesperson as he or she make the approach to each account more focused and effective.

Below is an example of a very basic account plan object that can help to drive that clarity of thought. It ensures that there is a clear strategy for the account and that key activities are being planned and executed during the year.

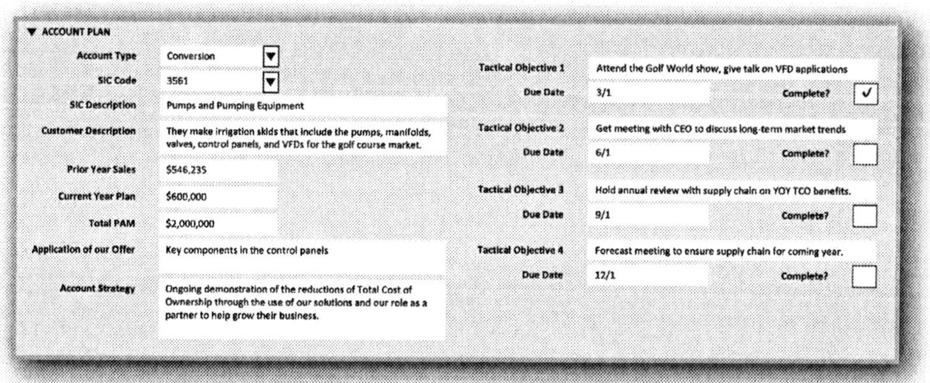
ACCOUNT PLAN

Account Type: Conversion
SIC Code: 3561
SIC Description: Pumps and Pumping Equipment
Customer Description: They make irrigation skids that include the pumps, manifolds, valves, control panels, and VFDs for the golf course market.
Prior Year Sales: $546,235
Current Year Plan: $600,000
Total PAM: $2,000,000
Application of our Offer: Key components in the control panels
Account Strategy: Ongoing demonstration of the reductions of Total Cost of Ownership through the use of our solutions and our role as a partner to help grow their business.

Tactical Objective 1: Attend the Golf World show, give talk on VFD applications
Due Date: 3/1 Complete? ✓
Tactical Objective 2: Get meeting with CEO to discuss long-term market trends
Due Date: 6/1 Complete?
Tactical Objective 3: Hold annual review with supply chain on YOY TCO benefits.
Due Date: 9/1 Complete?
Tactical Objective 4: Forecast meeting to ensure supply chain for coming year.
Due Date: 12/1 Complete?

(Figure 2.3.1)

The idea behind the tool is simplicity. What are the basic demographics of the account? What is our current business? What is our potential business? What do they do with our products or solutions? What is our strategy for the account? What are the tactics that we plan to execute to support that strategy? That's all.

Most account plans that I have seen are far more complicated than this, but at the end of the day, a simple plan like this is more likely to actually be fully understood and executed on by the salesperson.

To help give some clarity to your objectives, one way that you can think about an account is in terms of the number of products or services that you provide that customers are buying from your competitors.

Product available market, or PAM, is most often thought of as a strategic term for an entire market. Another way to think about an account is to view the PAM very tactically—as if the account itself were the market. In this case, we view the PAM in terms of products or solutions that we make that our customer is buying from one or more of our evil competitors.

This is the data that directly supports our definitions of conversion, extraction, and retention customers from chapter 2-2. The data is never going to be perfect, but it's meant to be directionally correct. There are multiple ways to estimate or secure the information for it.

At the most basic level, in the case of an OEM, if the salesperson has ever walked around the manufacturing line of the customer, he or she can see the competitive products in use and estimate their value relative to your own. If salespeople know how many machines are made a week, month, or year, they have an excellent basis to estimate your PAM.

That being said, there is absolutely nothing wrong with simply asking the customer. The worst that someone can say is that he or she can't tell you. Remember, you are just looking for an approximation here and not a precise amount.

On a tactical level, this is going to show the salesperson just how much existing business the customer has available. This can be used to set account objectives as well as priorities.

On a strategic level, this data can be invaluable for the marketing and product-management teams. Instead of market estimates, you will know with fairly decent accuracy how much business your competitors are selling into your account base.

For marketing, this allows for precisely targeted sales campaigns to be planned and tracked based just on customers that are buying product family X from competitor Y. For product management, product-feature priorities can be set knowing exactly how they will impact your ability to compete within your existing-customer base.

(Figure 2.3.2)

The intent here is, again, simplicity. The salesperson can select from the major product families that you sell, and indicate how much the customer buys of that product and from which competitors. That's it. To keep it simple for the salesperson, make it clear that you are not looking for an exact number, but just the approximate scale of how much they buy.

Your most significant accounts, which are commonly designated as strategic or key accounts, may have a deeper form of an account plan due to their importance and complexity. However, the basic structure of those plans should still be the same; know what the account is, what your strategy is, and what tactics you are executing.

For driving overall execution, a simple report can be created to show all of the fields from Figure 2.3.1 in one view so that you can see progress on the plans for all of a salesperson's accounts in one glance. One way to do this is with the account-activity scorecard that is shown in chapter 1-4. When you use any kind of tool like this to consolidate the information, the current state of progress will jump off the page.

You can also make the tool a bit more "live" by linking it to your ERP system to show YTD sales progress as a total or even by your product families. There is a real benefit to integrating that kind of reporting into the tool as it drives the salesperson back to the planning document. It brings the salesperson face-to-face with the strategy and tactics through the course of the year instead of just during the planning cycle.

Anything that you can do to make the planning document a living entity that is actually used through the year is going to ensure that you have more realistic plans that are adding value to the salesperson's life. It ensures that the salesperson is being proactive about the long-term development of customers.

KEY TAKEAWAYS:

- Account plans that actually get used are simple, tie to real-world activity, and remain as living, breathing documents while they are in place.
- Sales managers need to take the plans as seriously as they expect the salespeople to and follow up on their execution on a quarterly basis.

Chapter 2-4

Giving Your Salespeople the "Glengarry Leads"

In the opening of *Glengarry Glen Ross*, there is a great moment where Alec Baldwin's character holds out a stack of leads, neatly wrapped up with a gold ribbon and bow: "These are the new leads. These are the Glengarry leads, and to you, they're gold...and you can't have them...*because to give them to you would be to throw them away.*"

Anyone who has ever been a salesperson trying to find new business feels the power of that one line. Getting good, qualified leads to customers who actually have a reason to talk to you, is gold. Pure gold.

Sadly, they don't get treated that way by most companies and their sales organizations. I can't tell you how many times I have seen dealing with leads thought of as a nuisance by salespeople. A nuisance? Why? Because most of the leads that those salespeople are seeing have little more value than just handing them a phone book.

There are two things that define a good lead: how qualified it is and how timely it is. When I was a young salesman, we used to get what were called "bingo cards" from the various trade magazines in which we placed ads. Customers would send in some kind of a response card asking for more information, and then it was passed on to us to follow up. When I first started, I would enthusiastically chase each one. After a little while, it was more about being dutiful. Eventually, they turned into big piles that I threw away.

Why did that happen? Because the leads were not at all qualified, and they were far from timely. All that the card meant was that the customer wanted to see some literature on a product (remember, this was before the World Wide Web). Most of the time the lead did not really have an interest or a need to buy something. That's not a particularly high degree of qualification.

More importantly, all of these leads were old. By the time the card was mailed in by the customer, processed by the magazine, sent to my company, sent to the field, and assigned to me, at least a couple of months had passed. Oftentimes, once I finally called the customer, he or she could not even remember making the request for the information.

Much the same thing happens in today's advertising world. Most leads are in response to a request for more information from a website. They get processed by an agency, assigned some kind of score, and are then put into a queue to be followed up on. This no longer takes a few months, but it does normally take a week or more before it hits the salesperson—and the qualification issue still remains.

Many companies have found a good way to fix this by putting in a layer between the raw lead and the salesperson in which skilled telemarketers qualify and nurture the leads. If customers are just looking for information, the telemarketers send it immediately, but they also draw the customers out to get basic information on what they do and what their needs might be. The telemarketing team then nurtures these leads over time, keeping in touch with information related to those needs.

If and when the customer indicates that he or she would really like to speak to a salesperson, the lead goes to a salesperson for action. Believe me, once salespeople start getting leads qualified to that degree, they jump on them. No time is lost in taking action because the salesperson knows that this is a real lead—it's a Glengarry lead.

To think about this properly, we need to split leads into multiple levels of quality, with "quality" being defined as the level of qualification that has happened with the lead to date.

Raw Leads
These are the original leads that detail customers who expressed some kind of interest in the company. Typically, these are either responses to advertisements or requests for more information on the web.

Marketing-Qualified Leads
These are leads that have passed basic qualification criteria to be worthy of ongoing nurturing. After the initial request from the raw lead is responded to and qualification questions have been asked, marketing sets some kind of a scoring criteria that determines the leads that are going to be nurtured over time by the telemarketing team.

Sales-Qualified Leads
These are leads that occur when customers have expressly asked to speak with salespeople. Normally this is after some sustained period of nurturing by marketing, but this can also happen directly during the qualification of a raw lead if the customer is expressing strong interest.

How big this telemarketing/nurturing team needs to be depends on the number of leads that you have coming in, but you may be surprised at how small it can be. If you have the right type of people and they are trained well with the appropriate tools, they can handle a large volume of outgoing calls each day to both new and existing leads that they are nurturing.

They key thing to this approach is speed. The first returned call to a raw lead should always happen within one business day in a B2B (business-to-business) environment or just in one day in the B2C (business-to-consumer) space. Once a customer says that he or she wants to speak with a salesperson, the ideal response should come within hours but never after more than a day.

There are several companies out there that can help you to be very sophisticated with this approach, building the management into your CRM and applying a scoring methodology to every lead. I think that this kind of a system can be very effective but would caution you not to try to boil the ocean all at once if you are trying this for the first time.

If you are just starting, this would be my prescription:

> Use the native lead-management system in your CRM. You don't need to have anything too fancy, but you want to be able to keep track of the lead, keep all of the notes in one place, know to whom it is assigned to at any given time, and run reports to show any leads that are not being responded to inside your time windows.
>
> Put a few good people on the phone to handle the leads. Ideally, you should start with one or two experienced people and then build up a team around them. The initial qualification work can be done by less experienced people working off scripts and common sense, but the nurturing part of it is going to take more skilled staff.
>
> Sales managers have to be very firm in ensuring that their salespeople do their parts in responding to every lead in a timely manner. If you

> are going to do it, do it right. The signals that are sent as a leadership team have to be very clear.
>
> Be sure to have some kind of a feedback system for the leads in your CRM. You want to know what the quality of the lead was when the salesperson made the first call as well as what ultimately happened to each lead. This data needs to be constantly fed back to the marketing and telemarketing/nurturing teams to help refine the qualification system.

The great thing about this kind of system is that it gives a fast response to the customer while using the right types of resources at each progressive level of qualification. It might seem excessive to set up dedicated resources to do this qualification and nurturing, but it really comes down to the relative costs of the resources that you are using for each customer touch.

As a lead progresses through qualification, both its value and the skills required to handle it increase. For handling the early stage leads, it's not so much a question of "Can outside salespeople do this?" as "Should outside salespeople do this?" Outside salespeople are our most expensive means to touch a customer and should be used with leads only when they have the appropriate value. They are also never going to be quite as good at it as a dedicated team that does it all day.

Personally, I would rather have fewer salespeople and a small nurturing operation that does its job really well than trying to spread the function around the sales team and have the job done poorly.

Salespeople should certainly deal with leads; it's a core element of what they do. If sales managers want to make sure that they are helping their salespeople to be more effective, then they need to ensure that the leads that they are working with are the ones with which they will get the best return on the investment of their time.

KEY TAKEAWAYS:

* Effective leads are timely—in today's world, customers expect a response in hours, not weeks.
* The best lead-management practices have methodologies to nurture leads from the initial raw lead to a marketing-qualified lead and finally to a sales-qualified lead.
* The "Glengarry leads" are qualified to the point at which the customers have expressly asked to speak to salespeople.
* Salespeople should always be part of the continuous-improvement loop for leads in their organizations and provide feedback on all sales-qualified leads that they handle.

Chapter 2-5

Stopping Wasted Sales Calls

The sales call is the single most important thing that a salesperson does with his or her time. Salespeople are face-to-face with their customers and are conducting the most high-value interaction possible. It needs to be treated that way.

It's a sunny day in the early fall in Milan, Italy. I came to the area for a sales meeting with European channel partners and was now going to meet the president of a medium-sized machine builder that we were doing business with.

The local salesperson picked me up at my hotel, along with the regional leader to whom his boss reported. We drove through Milan traffic talking about all kinds of things. We talked about the weather, we talked about our families. We talked about soccer, we talked about the insanity in the world. We pretty much talked about almost everything you can think of.

We finally pulled up in front of the customer and get out of the car, and the salesman started leading the way to the gate…until I stopped him.

What's wrong with this picture?

We had talked about everything in the world except what we were about to walk into: a meeting with the president of a company, his senior staff, and two executives from my company who had flown in to see him.

We then held the planning meeting in the parking lot that we should have had on the way over, and we went on to have a moderately successful sales call. The president wanted to continue the dialogue and invited us to dinner.

I could not really believe what had happened before the sales call. We actually had a very well-defined system for planning sales calls, particularly joint sales calls, integrated into our CRM system.

It was not overly complex, just a few key questions to ensure that everyone was on the same page. The team members had been trained on it and knew that they were expected to use it. Everything was there; it had just not been used.

After we got into the car, I asked the salesperson why? Why, after all of the training that we had given on it and all of the emphasis on the importance of planning sales calls, had he not done it in this case—when he was going on a call with both the head of sales and his boss's boss?

He turned his head as he drove to look right at me and said, "Well, Salesforce.com, it just does not fit my style."

Out of the corner of my eye, I could see all of the blood drain out of the regional leader's face.

What would you say in that moment?

Certainly, several choice quotes from that scene at the beginning of *Glengarry Glen Ross* came to my mind, but I decided to go with patiently reexplaining not just that this was expected, but also how it was for the salesperson's own benefit.

It reminded me of the experiences of a doctor in *The Checklist Manifesto.* He had been working for years to get checklists used in the operating room. He could show clearly with empirical data that using a checklist literally saved lives by significantly reducing infection rates. Every doctor to whom he talked would look at his data, nod in agreement, and say what a good idea it was—and then not do it.

That's the challenge that sales managers face when they try to get sales-call planning done. The sales manager will explain it patiently and consistently, the salespeople will nod their heads, and then the salespeople will just keep doing what they have always done.

You see, they all agree that it's a good idea—for everyone else. "I don't need to plan a sales call. I've been doing this for decades!"

Sales managers are going to have to work hard to change this behavior. They need to keep explaining it over and over again—and not just accept it when the behavior does not change. As an old boss of mine used to say, "People respect what you inspect." Sales managers must set an expectation for this and then stay on top of it.

When someone is not planning their sales calls, or is just giving it lip service, it needs to be made clear that it's unacceptable.

At this point, you might be shaking your head and wondering why I'm making such a big deal out of this issue. Why does every sales call need to be planned? I believe firmly that the sales call is the single-most important activity that a salesperson engages in. Not planning it to some degree borders on professional negligence.

That being said, the plan itself has to actually add value for the salesperson. I'm not suggesting a complex and time-consuming task—just something simple to bring clarity to the salesperson's mind about what he or she intends to do when entering the room instead of just reacting.

I've seen all kinds of sales-call-plan tools and templates, and the degree of irrelevant detail in some of them boggles the mind. The goal of the plan should be to do nothing other than give the salesperson clarity about what to accomplish in the sales call—that's it. As long as the salespeople can look at the plan and see just that, they will view it as a tool that is there to help them.

Use caution as you design your version of this. Like so many other things in a CRM, people are going to have ideas about things that "would be nice to know" if they were in the tool. Resist this. The simpler the tool, and the more directly it applies to what the salesperson is going to do, the better chance you have of it being used in the manner you intend.

Does this have to be in the CRM? Not necessarily. If I knew with certainty that every salesperson was going through a basic checklist before every sales call, I would be pretty happy. That being said, if you are approaching your CRM as the operating system for your sales team and as a communications tool for all of the parts of the organization working with the customers, then there is a real benefit in doing so.

For me, the proper planning of a sales call boils down to just five questions:

What do I want to accomplish?

This is the overall end result that you plan to come away with from the sales call. It's what you are closing for. You might not be closing an overall deal, but in any sales call, you are closing for something—even if it is only the next sales call.

This may seem simplistic, but it really revolves around focus. No matter what comes up during the sales call, you can keep this objective in mind as long as it's clear and concise. Even in calls that may have a laundry list of specific tactical things that you want to get done, I would argue that they all still boil down to one overarching theme.

Often, this is an objective that is going to move a deal forward, such as "Secure a meeting with the head of engineering" or "Confirm the true sign-off authority for the deal." If it's early in the discovery process at a customer site, it could be as simple as "Agree to the next meeting." The key is to keep it short and simple so that there is no doubt in your mind about what the salesperson is working toward in the meeting.

<u>What information do I need from the customer?</u>

No matter what is going on in a sales call, there is specific information that you are planning to get during the course of it. In the spirit of simplicity, I don't think that it adds value to try and script the questions themselves; the best way to phrase a question is going to come up in the moment, and if you get too cute with memorized questions, it is bound to feel artificial.

"What is the budget for the project?" "Who has input to the specification?" "How is business looking for this quarter?" These classic qualification questions are all good examples of simple things that you would want to know but that you would probably say in a different way during the conversation.

Depending on the complexity of the sales call, this might end up being a bit of a list, which of course proves the point about the value of planning them out ahead of time.

What do I need to tell the customer?

Just as we have information that we need to get from a customer, if we are already working to understand some of the customer's needs, we also have information that we need to give. This can be as basic as a specification of a product or the delivery schedule for an order.

Having the checklist written out and ready ahead of time ensures that you don't forget to deliver any of it and can think out the context in which you want to deliver it during the call.

There is an additional benefit here that in compiling the list, you are likely to have a bit of an internal brainstorm session with yourself that will suggest other facts with which you might want to be ready.

Thinking of new questions to ask the customer during the call does not mess anything up, but information to give to the customer needs to be prepared ahead of time.

Naturally, some part of what you are going to tell the customer is going to be based on the information that was gathered with the previous question. The plan for the call should have that in mind if you can anticipate some of the possible responses. "Gaming out" the sales call like that is an excellent coaching activity for the salesperson to do with their manager.

What topics do I need to be ready for?

This is probably the best topic for that "internal brainstorm" that we just mentioned. Running through the call in your mind and anticipating questions or issues that may come up only helps you to be ready for them.

This question is particularly important in any kind of joint call to ensure that everyone on the call is prepped for any possible land mines—if only to just avoid stepping on them.

These are normally going to be about performance issues such as delivery or quality, but they could also involve more emotional topics like anger at, or distrust of, specific individuals.

No matter what the topic is, the old maxim of "Forewarned is forearmed" certainly applies.

Is there anything that I need to bring?
This is the most mundane of all the questions, but it is still important. Showing up without the requested technical information or proposal document can really kill the momentum of the call. Just taking a few moments to jot them down makes a difference. If there is nothing to bring other than your smiling self, that is fine too—just be sure of it.

If the call is going to be a joint one, then this kind of planning is even more important. Everyone in the meeting needs to know the plan so that people are not tripping over each other or inadvertently undercutting the messaging. For all of the questions above, each individual should know his or her specific role and what information to get or give during the call.

If you go back to the sales call in the story at the beginning of this chapter, you can see the problem that I was facing. I had absolutely no idea what I was expected to do in that room beyond saying "Hi, how are you doing?" I had no idea whom we were meeting with or what their agendas were. I had no idea of any performance issues that I might be on the hook to explain or apologize for. The most likely outcomes were that the call was going to either be a complete disaster or just a grip-and-grin meeting that was a waste of time for everyone involved.

Planning like this is also how you avoid the curse that my friend Joe fell prey to in chapter 1-4, where the manager just takes over the sales call. Occasions when it makes sense for the sales manager to take over the call are pretty rare. If the salesperson and the manager have talked through the five questions here and what parts each is going to fulfill, then they will both know exactly how they are going to play things in the room.

Keep in mind that no matter how well you plan a call, once you are in the room, something can come up that will toss the plan out of the window. However, if everyone is clear on the main objectives, then it is much easier for a salesperson or a sales team in the room to adapt as needed.

Here is an example of the kind of object that I am talking about that would be set up inside your CRM:

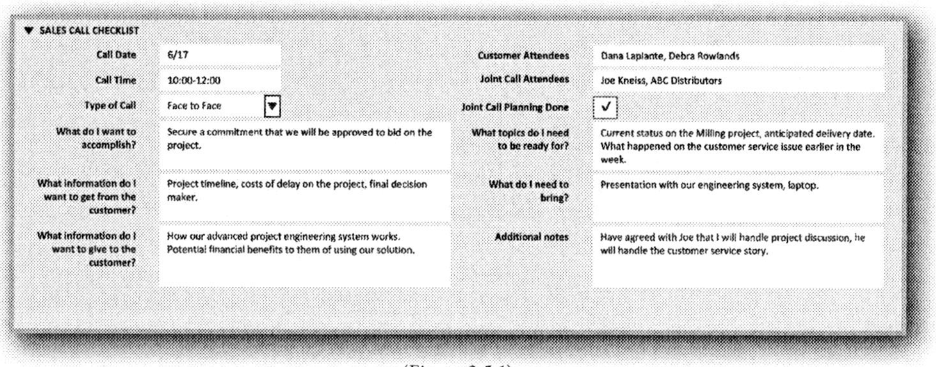

(Figure 2.5.1)

If you think about this object and how we are talking about using it, you will note that it does not involve a large amount of typing or clicking. The idea here is that the work goes into the thought, not the typing. The salesperson needs to have this plan established and review it right before the call to ensure that it is clear in his or her head and in the heads of any other people who are going into the room.

Even a plan like this may be more complicated than necessary. If it came down to it, the first three questions make up an effective basic checklist: What do I want to accomplish? What information do I need to get? What information do I need to give? If a salesperson has those fixed in mind, the call will run well.

All these questions are intended to do one thing: help the salesperson get clarity of thought to ensure that he or she gets the most out of the sales call. If you can just achieve that, simple clarity of thought before every sales call, you will have a huge impact on the effectiveness of your sales team.

KEY TAKEAWAYS:

* The sales call is the most important thing that a salesperson does.
* Sales calls are most effective when they are planned out in advance, particularly joint calls.
* A simple plan is best: What do you want to accomplish? What information do you need to get from the customer? What information do you want to give to the customer? What topics do you need to be ready for?

Chapter 2-6

The Golden Five Minutes

While how a sales call is planned and conducted is important, what really sets top salespeople apart from their competition is what they do right afterward.

> It was a cold spring day in Milwaukee and we had just finished up a tough meeting at a customer that was small to us at the time, but that had absolutely massive potential.
>
> The purchasing executive that we were working with was very tough and had coached his team to work the same way. My salesperson, Paul, had taken things as far as he could so he asked for some help to break the logjam. We brought in two of our Sales Vice Presidents to help us try to change the dynamic.
>
> Just to add to the fun, one of the VPs, Bill, was someone that I had worked for years before. He was a bit of a legend in our company and someone whom I had always wanted to impress (and was fairly sure that I had not.) I was probably feeling more pressure to look good in this meeting than my own salesman was.

After two long hours in the room, we finally made some real progress and wrapped up our meeting with pages of notes. Paul had done a great job leveraging the two VPs to create a conversation around what we might be able to do to add real value for the customer.

We all piled into the car for the drive back to Chicago. Bill and the other VP sat in the front and Paul and I sat in the rear. As we got going, Paul and I immediately started to debrief the meeting, running through the notes and the list of to-do items–talking through all of them.

I coached Paul on what he thought had gone well and poorly in the meeting, where he thought that we should go from here, and how he thought we should take care of all of the action items. It was clear that Paul had a crystal-clear map of where he was going and what he was going to get done in the next few days.

As we finished up, Bill turned around in his seat and looked back at both of us. He gave us one of those long looks where you tend to get really nervous about what it means. Then he turned his focus on me and said "Maybe you did learn something back when you used to work for me."

It was probably the best compliment that I have ever gotten.

What we had been doing during that car ride was nothing that we had invented. It's something that good salespeople have always done and that Bill had certainly done when I worked for him.

We were taking advantage of what I like to call the "Golden Five Minutes." Right after a salesperson walks out of a sales call and before anything else has been able to intrude on his or her thinking, the salesperson has the best sense of what just happened and what needs to be done about it.

In a joint call like this one, it's the ideal moment to provide coaching. In a solo sales call, it's the best possible moment for the salesperson to coach themselves.

Salespeople need to treat that time as the gold that it is and not pick up the phone or take on any other issues until they have done the basics. The salesperson needs to ensure that they don't drop any balls for the customer that they just saw. Even if the salesperson took extensive notes during the call, he or she probably had some items that did not get written down in the moment—particularly if they were bigger-picture items.

The operative words for what has to happen in that golden five minutes are *review*, *reflect*, and *redirect*.

Review

When salespeople get out of calls, they need to sit down somewhere private, such as in their cars. They need to take out their notes and look them over to check that they are correct and that they are not missing anything. It's hard to capture everything during a conversation in notes—particularly if you are trying to maintain eye contact. That's why getting it all down right after the meeting is so critical.

Reflect

During calls, salespeople are in active-listening mode and are reacting in the moment. That can get in the way of thinking about the big picture. As they review the notes, they are going to think of insights or actions that they would not have in the moment because now they are privy to everything that happened over the course of the entire meeting.

Whether the call was about a specific deal or just building a relationship, the salesperson has to sit back and think: "What should I be doing to keep moving this forward?"

> Reengage
> From both the meeting notes and the reflections on the meeting, the salesperson is going to have three lists of tasks: tasks that were committed to the customer, tasks that the customer committed to do, and tasks that the salesperson has since realized need to be done to drive things forward. That's the moment when things need to move from the notebook and the salesperson's head into the CRM.

Let's be realistic. The temptation is always to do this a bit backward—like the classic ready, fire, aim. The salesperson comes out of the call, grabs the phone, and starts calling people to get things done from the sales call or to report on the outcome to the manager or channel partner.

I'll bet a large amount of money that this is what most of your salespeople are doing today. They can and should still do that—just not until after they take those golden five minutes to review, reflect, and reengage.

That reengagement is one of the other areas in which your CRM can become a real tool to work on behalf of the salesperson. If you use it right, you can use it to both project manage all of the tasks as well as engage the broader organization in support of the salesperson.

The simplest way to do this is with the task function that is found in most CRM systems. When the salesperson leaves the call, and is moving into the reengage mode, the salesperson creates tasks in the CRM for every commitment that was made to the customer along with the deadline required to meet the date promised. The task is linked to either the account or the specific opportunity that it is related to.

If the salesperson is the one driving the task, he or she should self-assign it, but if the salesperson is going to rely on someone else in the organization, it should be assigned to that person. As far as the tasks that the customer committed, those should be assigned to the customer.

To make this really effective, it has to be done in the moment, right at the end of that Golden Five Minutes. How best to do that will depend on the specific CRM or tools that you are using. Most CRM tools have a mobile component designed to work on a phone or tablet that will work in a car right after a call. However, I've found that very few salespeople use them because they are not optimized for this activity.

Most of the tools out there are too complicated and take too many clicks to do these simple things because they are attempting to let the salesperson do in a mobile environment virtually everything that the CRM can do in a desktop environment.

One company that has taken a unique approach to this is tact.ai. The first time that I met Chuck Ganapathi, the founder, I felt like I had finally met someone in the CRM business who really got what a salesperson needed to function in the real world.

At tact.ai, Chuck's team approached the design of the company's mobile tool from the perspective of what the salesperson would want to do in the mobile context. Tact.ai makes getting those tasks done as simple as possible with a minimal number of clicks or taps.

Another way to approach the problem is by using a voice call. In the past, right after a sales call, a salesperson would call their internal sales-support resource and run down the list of tasks that needed to be done. They would agree on a plan to get them done and move on. With the changes in sales staffing in today's world, that option does not exist in most companies.

One company I worked with found a middle ground by creating a pool of people who were all logged in to the CRM so that the salespeople could call in and just tell them what to put into the tool after the meeting; they could change information on an opportunity, create a new one, update the account record, create tasks, or do just about anything that was needed while the salesperson had it all fresh in mind.

Today, companies such as tact.ai are deploying apps that act as bridges between a voice assistant and your CRM. This allows salespeople to just activate the app and dictate what they want done and have the app handle all of the typing and clicking. The whole idea is to make the data entry simple for salespeople so that they really do use the tool. That's how you can really drive adoption of a CRM for salespeople—by making using the CRM easier than any other way to do the job.

Finally, there is the follow-up to the customer from the call. No customer is ever going to complain about a salesperson who takes the time to send the customer a list of the things that have been committed at the end of a meeting, and customers will almost always appreciate it if it includes the commitments that they made themselves. It's a sign of professionalism and increases the likelihood in their minds that the salesperson will be following up on all of the items.

All of these tasks are going to start to add up, and we talk about a variety of ways to manage this in chapter 3-4. The central concept is that we are using the CRM as a task manager for the salesperson, and that will add value. The CRM acts as a project manager and helps the salesperson to plan the execution of all commitments.

If it's done right and really adopted by the sales team, the CRM ensures that the salesperson never drops the ball on a commitment to a customer. That's a real value.

A simple report that shows every commitment—whom it is for, which customer or deal it impacts, how much money it is worth, when it is due, and who is responsible to get it done—can drive a huge amount of customer satisfaction for your salespeople. Just think about how your customers will react when these commitments are always acted on.

Let me talk a bit more about assigning tasks to the rest of the organization. In general, this is one of the true benefits of using a CRM as it allows us to engage the larger organization in the selling process. Communication is simplified as all of the core facts to provide context around the task are right there in the account or opportunity object to which the task is attached.

The challenge is that while it is simple to assign the task to someone, it's not quite as simple to get that person to accept that task as a priority.

This is one of those times where we can get a better result by asking instead of telling. If the salesperson is creating a task for someone in the system, this should be combined with a phone call or e-mail asking for the help. Just what salespeople do case by case depends on their relationships with the resources and their management.

For more complex requests that will involve significant investments of time or money, just assigning a task to someone is not really going to be sufficient. The tool that I prefer to use for this is a "support request", which provides more detail and sends the request to the manager of the group that will be providing the resources.

Here is an example of what that tool looks like:

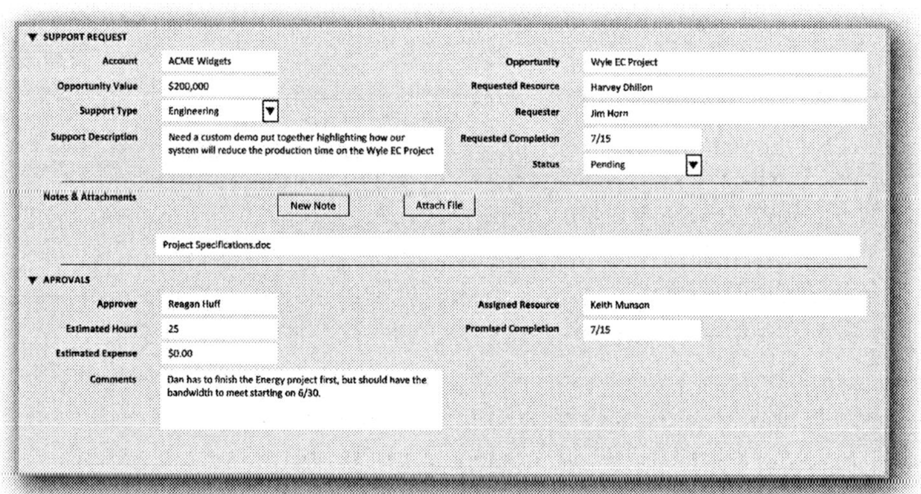

(Figure 2.6.1)

With this tool, the salesperson can request the specific resource or funding that they want and attach any notes or documents required to explain it. The manager of the resource gets to evaluate the request, estimate the work required, and approve or reject it; and if it is approved, the manager will assign a resource to it.

If the request is simple and is not going to use up much time or money, tasks are still the simplest tool. However, if the request is going to be substantial, the support-request tool ensures that you have full buy in from all of the stakeholders for the resource.

One item that you might want to separate from tasks or support requests is product feedback. It's unfortunate how often valuable product feedback is not used properly because it tends to come in anecdotal form. It takes real discipline for organizations to compile that information in a meaningful way that ties the feedback to the sales volumes involved with it.

If a salesperson gets feedback from a customer on a product issue or proposed feature, it can be very powerful to attach that feedback to the account or a specific deal as it clearly shows the revenue associated with it.

As more and more feedback comes in from different sources, product management ends up with a database of all the deals and customers tied to the various requests. When the department needs to justify the development of a feature or the modification of an existing product, a business case can be based on real data instead of just using estimates.

Then comes the really fun part. Once the feature or modification is done, the customers who gave the feedback can be contacted directly by the salesperson to roll it out. The customer gets to see that the feedback was listened to and acted on. Who would not want to go on that sales call?

Far too often, product feedback seems to either go into a black hole and be ignored, or it comes from one or two anecdotal cases that are then blown way out of proportion. This information can be absolute gold to an organization—but only if it is approached systematically so that all of the information is kept in perspective when it is used in the decision-making process.

If the CRM tool is used to tie product feedback systematically to specific customers or opportunities, the impact can be quantified and properly prioritized. This also allows management to ensure that all of these customer issues receive prompt and proper follow-up.

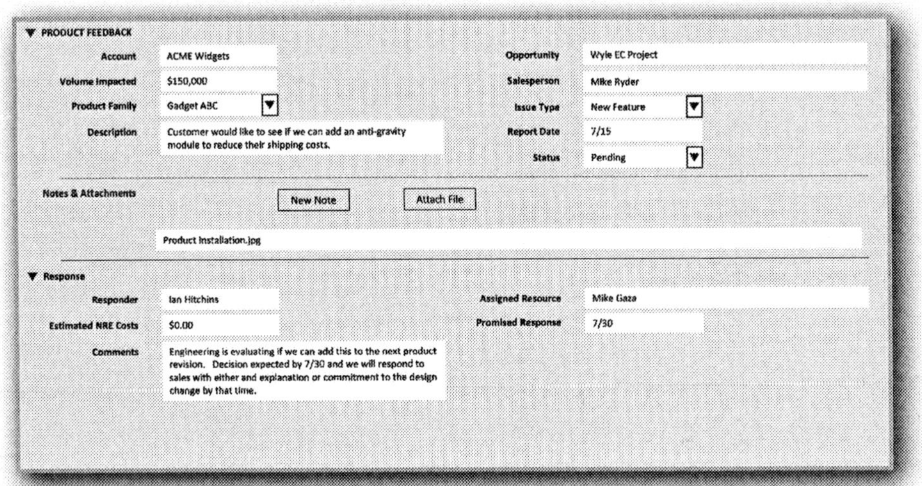

(Figure 2.6.2)

The tool gives the salesperson a simple way to indicate the customer and sales volume impacted, the product in question and the issue involved. The salesperson can attach notes or documents to provide deeper detail. In cases like this, pictures are always worth a thousand words. The product manager can provide a detailed response or assign a resource to dig deeper into the issue before making a decision.

These two items do add steps to the process and require modifications to the CRM, so you have to decide if they will add enough value to justify that. These tools will generate a much higher level of engagement from the rest of the organization as people get to have voices in how the request is handled.

As with tasks, simple reports can be generated on all of the outstanding-support requests that can help management balance workloads and identify parts of the organization that need help to better engage with the sales force and customers.

The bottom line here is that the salesperson who does a great job at following up on sales calls has a huge advantage over competitors. Why? Because as simple a concept as this is, most salespeople just don't do it. I've never met a salesperson who wanted to intentionally drop the ball on customers, but if there is no real system in place to manage it, those balls will be dropped. It's inevitable.

Without any modification, you can use any CRM to help your salespeople do it better. With some minor development of a few tools to integrate into your CRM, you can implement reliable ways to engage not just your sales force but your entire organization to help meet customer needs. The CRM then prevents the balls from being dropped by any of them.

When they look at your salespeople and your competitors, customers will see the difference.

KEY TAKEAWAYS:

* The first minutes after a sales call are like gold to a salesperson—if they are used properly.
* Those minutes are the best time for the salesperson to review the sales call, reflect on the best ways to move forward, and reengage on the tasks that he or she committed to the customer or has now added to the sales process.
* The task tool in your CRM can be used by the salesperson to project manage all of these activities and engage other people in the organization as needed.

* The support-request and product-feedback tools for a CRM can effectively engage the broader organization in response to more complicated issues raised during the sales call.

Chapter 2-7

Stop the Leaky Bucket

One of the most overlooked items that I see in most manufacturer-channel relationships is how unaware they are of something that I like to call the "leaky bucket."

> It was a warm spring day, and I was sitting in the back of a sectioned-off ballroom at a nice, high-end resort—the kind of place that big-industry meetings are held. That was convenient, as I was at a big-industry meeting.
>
> A few months before, I had taken over one of our sales teams and had spent the winter diving deep into our customer data to figure out what our best strategy going forward would be.
>
> Looking closely at the data had uncovered a pretty shocking statistic, and we were going to need to make a big change to our go-to-market model as a result.
>
> Most of our major-channel partners were attending the meeting, so we had gotten them to all agree to attend a breakout meeting at which we were going to fill them in on the findings. After the usual preliminaries, I got to the heart of the message.

"Folks, when I add up all of our mutual customers, we've dealt with about twelve thousand over the past ten years. That might sound great, but the reality is that all of those customers have been in a very leaky bucket.

"Of those twelve thousand customers, only about six thousand are still active customers today. Now, we expect a certain amount of customer loss every year, but what started out as a very small leak has been getting bigger and bigger every year.

"This year we are on track to lose 1,400 customers. I don't know about you, but to me, that is the kind of thing that can put all of us out of business."

That was the moment when I knew that I had their attention.

The bottom line is that we all have some degree of a leaky bucket in our customer base. This kind of "churn" is expected and is normally offset by new customers that that sales team brings in.

However, in the case above, the loss rate of customers far exceeded the rate of new customers coming in. No matter how many new customers that we put into the top of the bucket, if we keep losing more and more out of the bottom of the bucket every year, it is going to be a losing proposition.

After that meeting, we were able to admit that there was a problem and got to work on solving it. We did not come up with the best solution, but we were at least able to stem the flow of lost customers.

Here is where things get interesting. At the time, I assumed that ignorance of this very high loss rate was unique to that business. A few years later, when I looked at the numbers at my next company, I saw the same phenomenon. Then I then looked at adjacent businesses in the same company, and yet again no one had noticed the same high degree of churn. It was becoming clear to me that this was a common problem.

As important as any efforts that you make to get new customers into your business are, efforts to retain the old ones are just as important.

That might seem like one of the most obvious statements that you can make about sales, but none of these businesses were even tracking the lost-customer numbers when I first went to look for them. Everyone knew that there was some level of loss, but nobody had any idea of the scale that they were experiencing.

I don't think that there is a business out there that is happy to lose close to 10 percent of its customers a year. A certain amount of customer churn is expected, but how much is OK? If you can cut whatever your loss rate in half, what does that mean for your overall growth? Why is it that in virtually every business with which I looked at this number, nobody had ever thought to look seriously at it before?

The Pareto Principle really comes into play here. In most companies, 80 percent of the business tends to come from 20 percent of the customers, and that is where the foci of most sales organizations lie. The lost-customer population is primarily made up of smaller customers, so each individual loss gets almost no attention; these customers are hardly ever noticed. As small as those customers may be, it's the aggregate of all of them that really ends up hurting when it gets too high.

Because the largest customers are getting the attention of the outside-sales teams and management, the smaller accounts tend to get managed by customer service or channel-partner teams. By "managed," I really just mean "reacted to." If a small customer wants to buy something, the client calls in and places an order with customer service. Nobody is really paying any proactive attention to that small customer; the client is just thought of as part of the flow.

Those small customers don't really have more than transactional relationships with you. That means that when something goes wrong or a competitor comes along with a better offer, you never really hear about it—they just start buying from someone else. Sometimes this is masked even more, as the customer still buys a little bit from you. The volume just goes down gradually, and it never really hits anyone's radar.

Talk about a self-inflicted wound! If we can just get proactive with those customers, we can not only stop our buckets from leaking so much, but we can also uncover small customers who have the potential to be large customers once we learn more about them and the opportunities that they may have for us.

I can tell you this much about getting proactive with small customers: the least impact that I ever saw it have was to cut the loss rate in half. In other cases, the sales volume from this population of customers actually went up by as much as 10 percent—just from initiating proactive contact with this set of customers.

Doing this is relatively simple, but the work is hard. Instead of having customer service just reacting to small customers when they call with orders, customer service has to get proactive. That is going to be a significant behavior change in most organizations, and is likely to require slightly more staff. However, if you do the math, I think that you will find that those changes more than pay for themselves.

Here is my basic prescription for plugging your leaky bucket:

> Establish the target list.
>
> If you look at your overall population of customers and subtract the ones who are being actively called on by your outside salespeople, what is left over is the target list—regardless of how little they are buying. Oftentimes, when I see attempts at this, there is a lower threshold in revenue that creates a new but smaller population of customers who are not managed proactively. Don't let that happen. The only way to plug the holes in the bucket is to go after all of them.
>
> Once you get things really clicking, you might even go further and try to get to customers who have left in the past few years. It certainly can't hurt to try, and even if you don't get them back, you can learn something critically important—why they left you in the first place.

Set up the contact mechanism.
In a perfect world, dedicated telesales resources are going to be working these lists. If you are not ready for that, your existing customer service or inside-sales teams can take it on. The trick is to balance the loading on them to create enough bandwidth for them to make proactive calls. If you go down this path, the only way to ensure that the calls actually happen is to set daily or weekly quotas for proactive calls and then stick to them.

Maintain regular, proactive contact.
The first contact is going to go along these lines: "Thank you for your business. We just wanted to check in on how we are doing. Is there anything that we can be doing to better serve you?" Once that is done for the first time, it's going to get pretty old for the customer if that is all that is said on the call. Your marketing teams can be tasked to provide you with a steady stream of fresh, meaningful content as you keep the contact alive. Certainly, every time that you reach out to the customer, you should include the customer-service element from the first call; you just have to tell customers something new as well to be sure that they are getting something of value to them from the calls.

This is not going to be easy. To do it right, there needs to be a concerted effort to generate content that ties to the customer's business or application. If the team is just vomiting out random product data, the customer is going to start to tune those calls out pretty quickly. It's real work for the marketing or product-management teams, but the libraries that they build for this effort will be used by the sales force and channel with larger customers as well.

The big question here is who does this—the manufacturer or the channel partner? If you are the manufacturer, you are going to be very tempted to do it yourself and maintain complete control of the process. While this is certainly a viable path, it's a hard one to follow.

Most channel partners are going to reflexively view this as an invasion of their turf and possibly as a prelude to your cutting them out of the picture and taking on the business directly. If you go down this path, you will need to preempt that thinking and get the buy in from the channel partners to move forward.

The main reason for having the channel partner drive the customer contact is quite practical. The channel partner already knows the name and contact information for the person at each of these small customers who actually buy your product. Even manufacturers that do a great job of gathering point-of-sale data are rarely going to have that information. Unless the channel partner is completely brought into the strategy, the partner is probably not going to give the manufacturer that information.

Regardless of which party is taking on the telesales role, the information flow also has to be a two-way street. All of the intelligence that is gathered in these calls has to be shared in a timely fashion between the channel partners and the manufacturer. If you use a channel-partner portal on your CRM, that can often be the best means to ensure that the information is being shared in real time.

If the manufacturer is doing the telesales role (and if and when its telesales people uncover new business), there has to be complete confidence on the channel partner's part that it will be directed through this partner.

If the channel partner is the one doing the telesales role, the manufacturer needs to do everything possible to assist the channel partner in setting it up. From generating the lists of targeted existing or lost customers to delivering the libraries of messaging to use for ongoing contact, the manufacturer has a scale to deliver this that few channel partners do.

As an added bonus, channel partners are going to value any manufacturer that is giving them this kind of tactical assistance with their customers. This should result in increased mindshare with management and their sales teams for your product line—which is really the point of this chapter. The more value that you can get your channel partners to place in your line, the better force multipliers they will be for your sales force. Everybody wins.

KEY TAKEAWAYS:

* Careful watch need to be kept on the customer base to ensure that the "leaky-bucket" effect is kept to a minimum.
* Simply getting proactive with the population of small customers will significantly reduce customer churn and will yield increased sales.

Chapter 2-8

Treat Channel Partners Like Actual Partners

Many companies go to market via some kind of a channel partner, either as their primary selling engine or to augment the efforts of their own sales teams.

The first big company that I worked for was and is an absolute master of working effectively with channel partners. In the United States alone, it built a network of over 2,500 distributors that drove sales in the market and provided local inventory and services for their customers.

Combined with that company's own sales force, that made for a formidable combination.

Then came the time when this big company was taken over by an even bigger company. That bigger company was from Europe and had tried to get into the US market for years without much success.

They had a relatively small sales force, and the channel partners that the company had worked with just did not have the scale and reach that the more mainstream American manufacturers brought to bear.

> The company bought us for our channel to market and paid a hefty premium to get it. It was the first real lesson that I had in the value that a business would put on something that was relatively intangible.
>
> The explosive growth that was seen after the acquisition paid off that premium in just a few short years—and has been paying off for the company ever since. It's the clearest example that I have ever seen of the value of manufacturer-channel relationships when they are done right.

This is probably all too basic for most of our readers, but before we go too deeply into channel, let's briefly set the stage for what we are talking about when we use the term "channel partner." There are several different types of channel partners and models of how to use them, but in general, they are people or organizations that don't directly work for your company but that work on your behalf to sell your product into the market.

Regardless of the types of channel partners that they are, they all act as force multipliers for your sales teams.

The four most common types of channel partners are distributors, resellers, value-added resellers, and sales representatives.

Distributor

A distributor has a public, formal relationship with a manufacturer to sell its product. They take titles to the products, stock them, and make their money from the markup that they add to their purchase prices when they sell them to the end customers. The distributor sets its own selling prices and terms and conditions of sale.

Reseller

A reseller has all of the same elements as a distributor, except that it does not hold stock.

Value-Added Reseller (VAR)
A value-added reseller takes products from the manufacturer and adds features or enhancements to an overall package prior to selling it to the end customer.

Sales Representative
A sales representative (often referred to as a rep firm) promotes the sale of products or services in a specific territory or set of customers on behalf of a manufacturer. Sales representatives are paid commissions that are typically percentages of the sales in those territories or to their sets of assigned customers.

How to effectively work with each of these types of channel partners and the best way to deploy them in a market is worth several books on its own. That's not what we are going to talk about here. For our purposes, we want to discuss how the sales manager can work with both his or her own salespeople and channel partners to get the best result.

This starts with taking a closer look at exactly how your salespeople are working with your channel partners. I hate to say this, but far too often, what looks like a good salesperson from a distance is just someone who is following a good channel salesperson around and taking credit.

In an effective relationship with channel partners, there is a division of labor.

In some accounts, the manufacturer's salesperson is the primary seller and makes most of the sales calls on the customer independently while keeping the channel partner in the loop on all activities. This is normally at accounts where almost all of the business with the customer consists of the manufacturer's products of services.

In other accounts, the channel partner's salesperson is the primary seller and makes most of the sales calls on the customer alone, bringing in the manufacturer as needed. This is true of the majority of accounts as most channel partners are selling a broad array of products from their line cards to the customer, giving the channel partners more reason to be with the customers on an ongoing basis.

For either type of account, the channel partner and the manufacturer need to collaborate closely, and their respective salespeople need to trust and understand each other's roles at the account. This is another area where the partner portal of your CRM can help to drive communication on the details in real time.

Finally, we need to look at how to enhance the overall relationship with the channel partner. The last thing that a sales manager wants is to have salespeople mixed up in resolving disputes or handling politics with your channel partners.

Don't get me wrong, I live in the real world and know that the salespeople are going to have to do some of this. The sales manager can do a lot to keep this at an absolute minimum.

What you want to do is ensure that the channel partner always sees value in what you do as a manufacturer and wants to work with you as a priority on its line card. The good news is that there really are just a few key things that can help you to accomplish this:

1. Bring the channel partner leads.

There is no quicker way to a channel partner's heart than bringing new business. Manufacturers that do this consistently are viewed as true partners of the firm who are making a real, measurable investment in helping the firm to grow. It does not hurt to keep track of the business that your team has brought to a channel partner and go over it in your regular reviews but, if you are really doing it, you won't have to keep track—the channel partner is going to know that list even better than you do.

2. Have true salespeople working with the channel partner.

If your salespeople are viewed as bringing something to the party for the channel partner, then they are going to be valued. There is a simple metric for this—if the channel partner's salespeople are always asking your salespeople to go with them into their accounts, then you have it nailed. If they are not asking, then you need to find out why.

3. Create a real sense of fairness.

Nothing is going to push a channel partner away from a manufacturer more quickly than an environment in which it feels that it is being treated unfairly. In any business relationship, there are always going to be disputes between the parties, and how you choose to handle them has a huge impact on the long-term relationship.

The first step here is to create consistency. However you handle channel partner A on an issue, you had better be consistent when you handle the same issue with channel partner B. If you do that, the partner may not like the answer for the issue, but it will at least know that it was fair. If you don't already have a written channel policy that details how you will handle the major elements of your working relationship, then it should be a priority for you to get one in place. If you do have one, it's worth taking the time to ensure that it covers the issues that your sales team is dealing with.

If you do need to write a policy, don't do it in a vacuum. Create a representative committee of channel partners to give input and to review the document as it is developed. If you do this, even if they don't completely agree with the final document, the channel partners are going to know that they were heard as the policy was developed.

What should be in that policy? Here are just a few of the basics that you should have clear guidelines on:

* Discounting qualifications
* Inventory requirements
* Training requirements
* Certification requirements
* Dedicated-staff requirements
* Demo-equipment requirements
* Exclusivity definitions and guidelines for handling competitive lines
* Growth expectations
* Differences in rules for distributors, sales representatives, value-added resellers, and resellers
* How new channel will be added—what approvals are required, what the guidelines for approval will be, what the strategy and rules for overlapping channel is, and how existing channel will be notified or involved in the process
* How special pricing will be moved from one channel partner to another when requested by a customer
* How sales territories will be established and managed
* How selling out of territory will be approved and managed if needed
* What sales planning will be expected
* How customer marketing will be expected to be done and how any cooperative-marketing funds will be made available and administered
* How conflicts with any competing lines that the channel partner carries will be managed
* How penalties for transgressions from policies will be administered
* How termination of a channel partner will be determined, appealed, and administered

Documents like this should never be written in stone; they should be living documents that adjust with the times so even if you already have one, you should still have a representative committee of channel partners that advise you on the evolution of policy.

4. Make the channel partner feel heard.

Having channel partners on your policy committee is just a start. One thing that many manufacturers overlook is just what great resources their channel partners are to their business as advisors. Every one of them has been successful at building and running a business.

Your channel team should work constantly to genuinely engage your channel partners and take advantage of what they know. Regular meetings with all of the principals on the future of the business, feedback sessions for product management with their front-line sellers, and smaller advisory committees are just a few of the ways that you can more fully engage them in your business.

Finally, we should talk briefly about planning. As you have read this book, you may have noticed that I am a huge fan of planning—but only planning that is relevant and that is actually going to be used. If you are going to set a plan with a channel partner, it needs to be something that you are both going to work together on and not just be a binder that gets stuck in a drawer after you leave the branch manager's office.

Sadly, most channel-partner planning that I have seen has resulted in long, detailed forms that get reviewed once at the beginning of the year and then put in a drawer and never looked at again until the following year.

I will never forget the awesome example of my late friend Richard Odle, who used to tape a twenty-dollar bill to a page in the middle of the binders that he sent to his boss. He was always able to safely retrieve the money later in the year when he visited his boss's office at headquarters.

This is where the CRM becomes an excellent tool as it not only allows you to keep the relevant data live but also allows for tracking of the tasks inherent to the plan to help the responsible salespeople ensure that they get done proactively.

Below is an example of the kind of channel-partner-planning tool that you could put into your CRM.

The intent of this object is just to cover the basics. We show some key metrics on performance, give some data on capability and compliance, and then lay out the core tactics that we plan to execute.

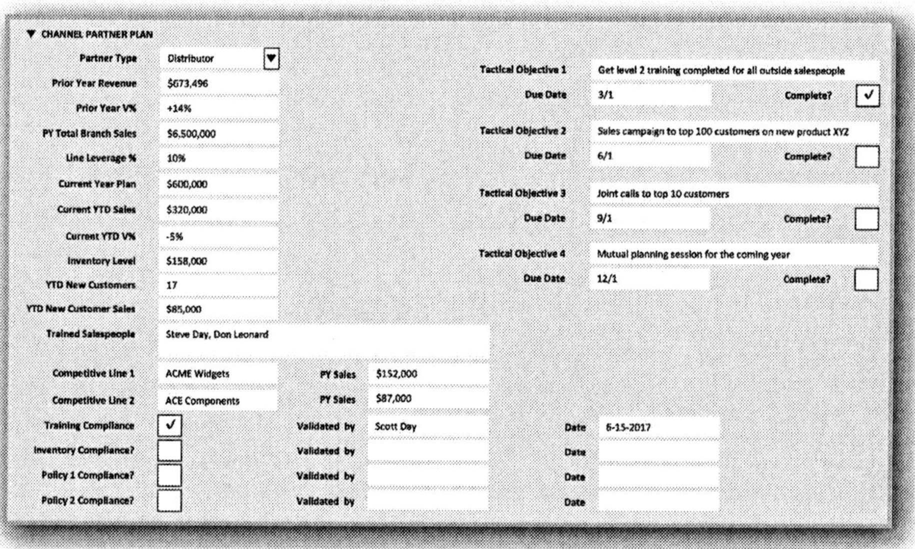
▼ CHANNEL PARTNER PLAN
Partner Type: Distributor
Prior Year Revenue: $673,496
Prior Year V%: +14%
PY Total Branch Sales: $6,500,000
Line Leverage %: 10%
Current Year Plan: $600,000
Current YTD Sales: $320,000
Current YTD V%: -5%
Inventory Level: $158,000
YTD New Customers: 17
YTD New Customer Sales: $85,000
Trained Salespeople: Steve Day, Don Leonard
Competitive Line 1: ACME Widgets — PY Sales: $152,000
Competitive Line 2: ACE Components — PY Sales: $87,000
Training Compliance: ✓ — Validated by: Scott Day — Date: 6-15-2017
Inventory Compliance? — Validated by — Date
Policy 1 Compliance? — Validated by — Date
Policy 2 Compliance? — Validated by — Date
Tactical Objective 1: Get level 2 training completed for all outside salespeople — Due Date: 3/1 — Complete? ✓
Tactical Objective 2: Sales campaign to top 100 customers on new product XYZ — Due Date: 6/1 — Complete?
Tactical Objective 3: Joint calls to top 10 customers — Due Date: 9/1 — Complete?
Tactical Objective 4: Mutual planning session for the coming year — Due Date: 12/1 — Complete?

(Figure 2.8.1)

This tool follows the same basic pattern as the account plan. We get the essential demographics and sales performance of the channel partner along with the tactical plan for growth to be executed in the year to come. What is added in are fields to record the status of the most common compliance issues that manufacturers expect of their channel partners, along with a record of who validated them and when. This can be important as those compliance matters often tie directly to financial benefits that are provided to the channel partner.

All of the activities laid out in this chapter are designed to help your salespeople; they won't have to worry about managing any of this if you are doing it as the sales manager or providing tools to make them simpler. The salespeople are going to wind up with better channel partners that help them sell more, fewer lost customers to make up for, and the ability to focus on what they have to do to support your strategy and just sell.

KEY TAKEAWAYS:

* Channel partners (distributors, resellers, value-added resellers, and sales representatives) represent one of the best force multipliers available to a sales team—if they are engaged as partners.
* To work effectively as a partner, a manufacturer should bring leads, have true salespeople working with them, create a real sense of fairness, and make the channel partner feel heard.
* As with customers, planning is effective only if it is set up to be used and reviewed regularly; otherwise, it just ends up in a drawer.

Chapter 3

Process

In 2017, businesses are expected to spend $37 billion on CRM software.

A shockingly large percentage of that $37 billion is being wasted.

Why? Because, as prevalent as they have become in today's business world, most CRM systems are being implemented 180 degrees in the wrong direction. The output from these CRMs is aimed at sales management, not the salespeople.

That's crazy.

The only way that we can get a return on the investment of that $37 billion is if salespeople use the tool to generate more revenue. That only happens if the salespeople truly adopt the tool into their daily lives, not if they are just complying with company directives to input data into the tool.

No matter how well the CRM tools are designed, no matter how good the software is, no matter how easy it is to use, it changes nothing if the salesperson does not make it an integral part of daily life. To make that happen, the salesperson has to see that, in exchange for the data that he or she is inputting, the CRM is giving back real intelligence that will make the salesperson more effective.

The irony here is that this is precisely what CRMs are designed to do—it's just not how most companies implement them.

Ask yourself this question: If you took your CRM system away from your salespeople, would they threaten to quit, or would they buy you a drink?

If you answer is the former, you can save yourself some time and stop reading right here, but if your answer is the latter, then this chapter is for you.

So why would your salespeople buy you a drink for getting rid of your CRM system?

Because to them, it is just a burden. It represents tasks that they have to perform to keep management happy, but it gives them no value back. The typical response that salespeople get when they put information into their CRMs is that the results are not good enough—they need to "row harder" and get better results.

The implementations of most company's CRM systems are simply not focused on helping their salespeople to perform better.

In this chapter, we are going to give detailed solutions around a process that will allow sales managers to use their CRM systems to deliver value to salespeople. We will show you how to use your CRM system so that when salespeople put data in, they will get information and insights back.

How do we do this? With predictive analytics and a coaching mentality for the sales managers. By applying predictive analytics to the data in the CRM, we can show the salesperson the best deals to focus on. Over the past several years, I have worked closely with a company called Alpine Metrics to do just that and the results were so remarkable that they were one of the primary inspirations for me to write this book.

The technology that Alpine Metrics has developed is powerful. They use an AI built upon Cortana Intelligence. It uses Microsoft Azure Machine

Learning to scan a historical data lake of won and lost deal activities in your CRM to accurately predict the results of the deals that are still pending. They also use the Microsoft Cognitive Services API to power a chat bot and provide a simple mobile interface for the salesperson.

Using Alpine Metrics, we can show salespeople the deals that they have that have the best chances to close, as well as any deals that are actually at risk. With tools like these, the sales manager can coach salespeople on how to separate the noise from the signals in their pipelines.

Some of this process is going to be about specific tools or features that you will enable in your CRM. Some of this process is going to be about the benefits of creating a historical database of your CRM data and integrating predictive analytics. Those are both important elements, but they pale in comparison to one simple thing—changing the mind-set of how you and your salespeople think about your CRM.

If you change the focus of your CRM to serve your salespeople, you create a virtuous circle. The more the tool gives back to the salespeople, the more they will use it, and the better the data in it gets. The better the data gets, the better the insights become for the salespeople.

As an added bonus, you still get all the management reporting that you want, and the data in it is far more accurate. However, you get that improvement in reporting not by driving compliance but instead by making the tool so valuable that your salespeople truly adopt it into their daily operating rhythm.

Chapter 3-1

The Machine

For years, my teams and I had been developing all kinds of individual elements of a sales process and putting them into place. We had all the key components of coaching our salespeople on deals and managing our pipeline, but we always struggled with finding the right way to talk about it to people outside our team—until I realized that the answer was right there in the very control systems that we were selling.

> I was sitting in a big conference room while Rich, the head of product management, pitches our latest and greatest technology to our channel partners. It had been a while since we'd had any truly new technology that these guys could drop on their feet, so it's a tough room.
>
> Just as Rich got into the meat of things to set up what our new technology would offer, he gave a basic review of what a control system does, in a continuous loop:
>
> "It **sees** what is going on by connecting to various sensors via its inputs."
>
> "It **thinks** about what to do in response to that using its programming."

> "It **does** what its programming dictates by connecting to various devices via its outputs."
>
> "**See-think-do.** Nothing revolutionary there. It's the basis of how control systems have worked for as long as they have existed."
>
> Rich was a pretty compelling speaker, and he was about to go into some genuinely cool stuff, but at that moment I had a bit of an epiphany and suddenly started to ignore Rich's presentation and make sketch after sketch in my notebook.
>
> You see, for the past few years at a couple of different companies, I had been working with my teams to develop many of the tools that you have and will read about in this book.
>
> At the time, they were a group of useful but disparate elements. As Rich was talking, I realized that they were all elements of a control system—one that was controlling the sales process that yielded our revenue.
>
> For the first time, I could see it all coming together as a cohesive whole: see-think-do. Our sales process as a machine for creating revenue for the company.

If you have a solid approach designed into your CRM for each of these elements, then you can build it all into what I like to call "The Machine." It's an overall process using see-think-do that keeps you and your sales team on a path of making the number over and over again.

For the purposes of this exercise, we will talk about a team that is solely measured on orders, but the same principles can be applied to teams that are measured on revenue or a combination of the two. Here is an overview of how it all works. We will go into more detail on each element later in the chapter.

See

To see what is going on, you have to be constantly evaluating the status of the team. Your central thought as you do that evaluation is to drive accountability to each and every individual on the team.

Oftentimes when teams make their numbers, they make them due to the heroic efforts of just a few team members—usually the same one or two people every time. There are a few people who miss plan by a mile, and then there is a population that I like to call the "mediocre middle" that either makes or comes close to achieving their plans, but never exceed them.

The more people on the team who are beyond, at, or close to plan, the better chance that you have of making the number overall. You have to create a culture in which every single person feels a personal responsibility to make his or her number. When someone misses it, the person has to genuinely feel that he or she let the teammates down and will go out of the way to make up the difference going forward.

That's why when we talk about seeing, we are not just talking about the overall result, but about ensuring that we have visibility into what is going on with every single salesperson that contributes to that result.

To do this effectively, you have to do more than just make the results visible at the end of the period. By that point, it's too late to help the salespeople to change things. To truly *see* where you are, you need to show what kind of path each and every salesperson is building toward the result. That way, the sales manager and the salespeople on their team have time to make it better.

In chapter 3-2, we will discuss some more sophisticated tools for looking at this, but for now, let's start with a very basic view of a team working to make numbers for the period.

▼ TEAM SUMMARY

Salesperson	Closed	Plan	Gap	Gap Close Deals	Gap Close Value	Manager Notes
Made Plan						
Jamie Whitcomb	$1,300,000	$1,000,000	0	3	$96,000	All three deals look very possible.
Diane Morando	$830,000	$775,000	0	5	$177,000	Wood Company deal ($110K) has strong chance.
Path to Plan						
Scott Walters	$900,000	$1,100,000	$200,000	7	$565,000	Pong deal ($384K) will be key to making it
Dave Henrichs	$865,000	$1,000,000	$135,000	6	$361,000	Foresight deal ($114K) needs help to close
Mark Mancini	$1,045,000	$1,100,000	$55,000	15	$485,000	Could go long on plan – get extra help on 5 deals with Smythe
Saralyn Luehrsen	$825,000	$900,000	$75,000	3	$227,000	ACME deal ($100K) is best shot. Needs T&C help.
Risk to Plan						
Bob Rochford	$700,000	$1,000,000	$300,000	5	$350,000	Needs to close every deal to make it
Tom Gerbo	$950,000	$1,200,000	$250,000	7	$300,000	Smith ($95K) and Tech ($100K) deals can get most of the way
Jackie Prescott	$600,000	$800,000	$200,000	6	$275,000	Need to pull in more deals to gap close.
No Path to Plan						
William Loman	$600,000	$900,000	$300,000	4	$210,000	Can minimize damage with Metro deal ($100K)
TEAM TOTAL	$8,615,000	$9,775,000	$1,160,000	61	$3,046,000	Need to close 38% to make plan

(Figure 3.1.1)

A view like this makes it very simple to drive accountability with the individuals while also showing clearly the paths that the salespeople on the team can take to making their overall quotas. Let's define some terms:

Closed is the total value of deals that have already been closed by the salesperson for the period.

Plan is the quota for the period

Gap is the amount that still has to be closed by the end of the period.

Gap-close deals are the subset of pending deals that the manager and the salesperson have agreed have the best chance of closing between now and the end of the period.

To understand if the salespeople have enough gap-close deals to make their plan, we also we have to know the average closure rate on deals for each salesperson or the team overall. Let's keep the math easy and for this example assume that we are talking about a team that has an average closure rate of 33 percent, meaning that team members close one out of every three deals in their pipeline.

That means that for a salesperson to have a reasonable path to making plan, he or she needs to have three times as much potential revenue in gap-close deals as the current gap to plan.

With that as the setup for each salesperson, salespeople are then sorted into one of four different groups:

> **Made Plan**: They already have enough deals closed to make the period. Every additional deal that they close is upside.
>
> **Path to Plan**: They have at least three times their gap in gap-close deals. Historical performance makes it likely that they will make their plans.
>
> **Risk to Plan**: They have between one and three times their gap in gap-close deals. They have theoretical paths to making their numbers but will have to close a higher percentage of deals.
>
> **No Path to Plan**: They have less than their gap in gap-close deals. They either have to focus on more deals from their pipelines as gap-close deals or do their best to minimize the damage.

The point of all of this is to give focus to the team. Does the team have a clear path to make its number? The CRM needs to be designed to show this clearly to each salesperson. Salespeople should be able to see this kind of view easily at any given moment.

If the salesperson does not have a path to make his or her number, then the salesperson can use the tools in the *think* phase to help find that path.

Think

Once we know where the problems are, we have to do more than just yell at the salespeople without a path to plan to "row harder!" When faced with gaps to their plans, most salespeople are going to focus either on their largest deals or the ones that they "feel" best about to try and close their gaps.

With predictive analytics like those developed by Alpine Metrics, we have the ability to take advantage of all the data that the salespeople have been putting into the CRM and deliver meaningful intelligence to them. That intelligence can help them to make much more informed decisions about the best deals to focus on.

Alpine Metrics has developed a focus-deals tool to help a salesperson or manager identify the best possible deals for closure in the current pipeline.

Focus Deals ×

Show: Above Ceiling Deals ▼ Manager: Bill Hughes ▼ Stage: *Any* ▼

	Deal Name	Owner	Amount	Score	Close Date
🔍	Dynasoar Flight System	Tony Dennis	$156,004	99	28-Apr-2016
🔍	Stockton WWTP – Phase 2	Finn Schenck	$120,000	97	09-Jun-2016
🔍	Pack-Tec Shrink Wrap Pilot	Dawn Bodinet	$209,354	96	15-May-2016
🔍	Compton Controls Q3 Pre-buy	Dale Gilkey	$164,566	95	31-May-2016
🔍	Bionic Systems – Left Arm	Ken Towsley	$322,000	92	23-Jun-2016

(Figure 3.1.2)

The AI of their predictive-analytics engine uses a wide variety of attributes showing how a deal has progressed over time to score its probability of closure with a high degree of accuracy.

This allows the salesperson or manager to use real science to determine which deals to focus on to close the gap instead of just pursuing the largest deals or going with a gut feeling. The tool also allows salespeople to take closer looks at deals that they are counting on with which the predictive analytics show risk.

This is one of the single most meaningful ways that a CRM system can give back real intelligence to a salesperson. Alpine Metrics has developed an approach that goes beyond the simplistic deal scoring that you may see in many platforms because their algorithm learns from how *your* team and *your* business actually progresses and wins deals.

The score that they provide is based on a historical database of your actual deal data and has far more meaning than just looking at basic data like the last time a deal was updated.

Do

Once the focus deals have been identified in the *think* phase, everyone, from the sales manager on down, needs to focus on driving the execution of those deals.

Although this seems fundamental, very few sales organizations take advantage of the functionality of their CRM to help them with execution. Even without special modifications, all of the major CRM platforms have features like tasks, which can be attached to deals and used to drive execution across the organization—making it far simpler for the salesperson to manage their overall pipeline and increase the momentum of individual deals.

When the salesperson or sales manager looks at every deal, he or she should always think about four key questions:

> What is the next actionable step for the deal, and when should it be completed?
>
> What help is needed on the deal? From whom? By when?
>
> Is there risk on the deal? If so, what is the plan to mitigate it?
>
> What is the closing strategy for the deal?

These questions and the plans that tie to them can all be embedded in the CRM for every deal. When this is compiled for all of a salesperson's deals, the CRM can give the salesperson a prioritized view of just what needs to be done and when to keep all of the deals moving. Used properly, this allows the salesperson to ensure that they never lose track of the tasks that need to be done that day to move their deals forward.

The beauty of using a CRM in this manner is the way that it can help drive the right coaching dialogue around individual deals. This is one of the most positive ways that sales managers can engage with their salespeople.

Advise

While the see-think-do loop is the core process that the sales team is running, the rest of the company gets tied into the process from an adjacent loop, called the *advise* loop. In control terms, this is a supervisory loop that runs apart from the main process and offers larger insights at a slower rate than the regular updates from controls running the core-control loop. (and yes, that sentence is totally controls geek speak)

If we really want to do it all right, we have to engage the rest of the organization on these deals. This engagement creates the advise loop. You want to build a culture in which you have sent a clear message to the organization that you consider every single person in the company to be a part of the sales team, and a part of this loop.

The actions of everyone in the company impact the customer in some way—and can help to close and win deals. We can use our CRM to drive their engagements in a highly effective way as they add information and assistance from outside of the normal control loop of the sales process.

This is where tools such as support requests, large-deal reviews, and the deal room come into play. They are all discussed in detail in other parts of the book, but all of them share the common theme of driving the engagement of the rest of the organization in deals.

Once you put all of this together, then you have built The Machine.

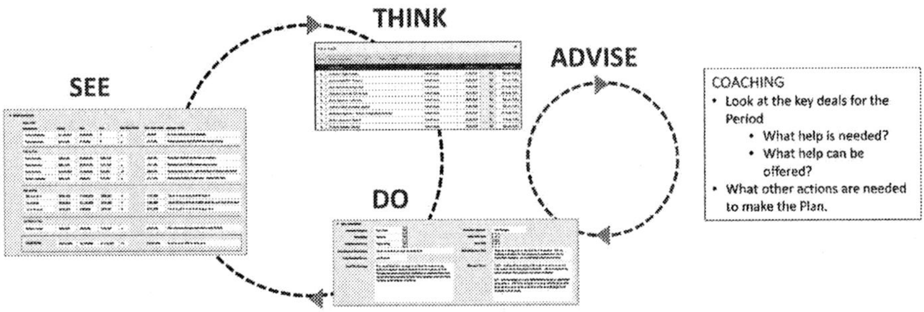

(Figure 3.1.3)

See-think-do and *advise.* If you combine a focus on proactive selling, rigor of execution, predictive analytics, and the engagement of the larger organization, then you have a machine that will allow you to continuously get the best possible result from your sales team members—by helping them to perform better.

The rest of this book is organized around those four pillars of see, think, do, and advise and how you can use your CRM and predictive analytics to make their benefits real for your salespeople.

Chapter 3-2

See

Before we can talk about doing anything with our pipeline, we first have to be able to see it clearly.

Way back when I was a front-line salesperson in San Francisco, I was sitting in my lovely beige cubicle banging away on what passed for a computer in those days when I got a very interesting phone call from the head of price management for our region.

"I'd like to bring a few people from Nashville in to see you next week."

"I'm sure that I can be available, but what in the world do they want to talk to me for?"

"Well, we've been looking at the numbers, and you've got one of the best deal-closure rates in the region. Nine out of ten times, when you negotiate a deal, you close it. We want to see if we can figure out how you do that so that we can replicate it."

"Nine out of ten? That has got to be wrong."

"No, seriously, we are sure it's that high."

"High? I mean that has to be low—it should be close to 100 percent."

"What?" (Imagine the incredulous tone of someone hearing such arrogance.)

"You know that getting deals into the system is a real nightmare—each one is a ton of clicks and typing, even if it's simple. I only put deals into the system when I absolutely must get a price approved before entering the order. Before that, I just keep track of them in my files."

"Oh." (Imagine the disappointed tone of someone having the floor fall away beneath them.)

"Are you sure that the folks from Nashville are going to want to fly all the way out west just to hear that?"

This was before the days of CRM systems, and this homegrown system was our company's first attempt to get a system-wide look at all of the pending deals that the sales organization was handling. Unfortunately, this system was designed to get order entry working for manufacturing and price management working for the product teams.

What it was not designed to do was to add anything to the sales process.

The sales teams all worked the system into our personal workflows as best we could, but it clearly was not matching what the designers intended. We were not trying to be subversive; we just did not see this as a tool that was going to help us in the selling process. We just used it for what it was good for—getting pricing approved and entering orders.

The company leaders thought that they were getting an overall view of their pipeline of deals, but they were really just getting a view of a small portion of it.

That's why the manner in which you roll out your CRM system is so important. If you can ensure that your salespeople see how it is going to help them in their jobs rather than other parts of the company, then they are more likely to truly adopt it rather than just comply with your requirements for it.

One of the ways in which this can have the most impact on salespeople is in helping them to *see* a clear view the pipeline. Take the story above. I was keeping track of dozens of deals in paper files. I had a stack of manila folders and relied on my memory to ensure that I was on top of all of them and following up when I should have.

I thought that I was doing a great job of this, but the reality is that I was dropping the ball all over the place. I had to be.

The irony is that for the same reasons that I had to have been dropping the ball, I had no idea how often I was doing it. There was no system to give me an overall view of my pipeline and where every deal was. My sales performance and hit rate were "good enough," so no alarm bells were going off.

I just know today that I could have sold far, far more than I did if I only had some way to ensure that I was never dropping those balls and was working each deal proactively.

That's how you have to explain the benefits of your CRM to your sales team. Your CRM software is the salespeople's best tool to ensure that they are proactively managing all of their deals. The sad reality is that since most salespeople don't do this well, it can be a serious competitive advantage for your team members if they do it.

Before we talk about the ways that we can use the CRM to let a salesperson see the pipeline, we need to talk about the data itself. Ask yourself this question:

How much garbage is in your pipeline today?

Keeping a pipeline healthy requires a continuous pruning of dead or improbable deals. One of the undesired side effects of measuring salespeople on the size of their overall pipelines is that they will never meet deals that they don't like, and the pipeline is inevitably inflated with deals that have no real chance of closure.

This has a very real and very negative impact on the salespeople. While they might feel good about having larger overall pipelines, filling it up with unrealistic deals causes them to lose our most critical factor for successful salespeople—focus.

You probably already have your best salespeople doing good jobs of this on their own as they innately understand the value of focus. The salespeople who are not doing it need to be coached over time to do it properly, and the key to that coaching is the set of questions that managers use when talking to them about their deals.

Over time, simply by consistently asking these questions, sales managers will train their salespeople to do this for themselves.

Here are the most important areas to probe when determining if a deal is viable.

> Age
>
> Depending on your typical sales cycle, there is going to be a point at which the probability of closing a deal gets to be very, very low. How do you know where this is? Take a look at your own deal data.
>
> When you do this, resist the temptation to go crazy with the data. In a huge sales organization, there can be some value to have a black belt come

in and break down the statistics, but in the small team environment that we have been focusing on, it's just going to confuse the issues.

Keep in mind, in this case, we are not trying to build a model of predictive analytics. We are just trying to come up with a reasonable set of filters that you can use to question the viability of deals and get the junk out of the pipeline.

The simplest way to go is to just look at the average time at each sales stage for three separate populations of deals:

* All deals in the current pipeline.
* All deals that have been won in the past year.
* All deals that have been lost in the past year.

When you look at the total age of deals that are won or lost, there is going to be a point where the chances of closure will drop like a rock. When you see deals past that age, the coaching question for the sales manager is a bit obvious:

> This deal is getting pretty old—what makes you feel like it's a real deal for the customer?

That does not mean that you need to kill every deal over that age—some of the best deals that I have seen have been long-life ones—but they are exceptions, and salespeople will need to be able to make compelling cases to convince their manager to keep such deals in the pipeline.

Length of Time in the Sales Stage

The total length of time that a deal has been around is one thing, but how long it has been at various sales stages can be even more telling. This is why in the analysis discussed above, we wanted to get the data for each sales stage and not just the total time to closure.

The average time at any stage for won deals is going to be your target, and for each of these stages, the times for lost deals are likely to be longer—normally much longer. That gives you a range to use to know where you should be questioning deals.

As with total life, just because a deal is taking longer than normal does not mean that it is automatically junk; it just means that the salesperson needs to be able to explain clearly why it is taking longer and what is being done to keep it moving.

Some good coaching questions around these deals could be:

> This deal has been stuck in the negotiation stage for some time. Why do you think that is?
>
> If you could wave a magic wand, what would it take to get this deal moving again?

In addition to helping you to find areas to coach your salespeople, this stage data can help you to uncover issues with your back office. For example, if deals are getting stuck for a long time at the quotation stage, that can be more due to internal issues in your own company than the customer.

When several of the same issues come up, it's the sales manager's job to get with the organizations in the company where those issues are and work with their leaders to solve it for your salespeople.

Decision Maker

One of the toughest things to determine on any deal is the identity of the real decision makers at the customer. This is not entirely on the salesperson as the reality is that people always have egos and the ones dealing with your salespeople will often identify themselves as the decision makers. It requires skillful questioning on the part of the salesperson to determine whether this is true without irritating the person who is representing him or herself as the decision maker.

For our purposes here though, the sales manager is the one who has to do the skillful questioning to see if the salesperson really knows and is dealing with the person who will ultimately sign off on the deal. One approach to this questioning is to go down the hierarchy path:

> For whom does this person work? Does the person's boss have to sign off on any part of this?
>
> Are there other employees of the customer who have input on the decision? Which ones?
>
> Have you met with the key people? Do they have even informal input on the final decision?

If the salesperson can't quickly answer these questions, the deal has a lot of work to be done. However, this can also be a great coaching moment for the manager to help the salesperson think through the kind of mapping that he or she should already have done to find the real decision maker.

It won't take too many coaching sessions like that before the salesperson starts to beat you to the punch and gain more skills at deciphering the maps of political power in the customer accounts.

If you deal with large or complex accounts, it can be well worth investing in the kind of specialized training that companies such as Revenue Storm offer in uncovering and mapping that political power.

Dollar Amount

Considering the variety of bills of material that my salespeople have dealt with, I've always been amazed at how many deals are out there that are exactly $100K, $500K, and $1 million. While that kind of rounding is fine in the early stages of qualification, it should almost never be the case once a deal has been quoted. If it is, it's really a red flag that the salesperson is not working the deal at a detailed level with the customer—the proposal scope or bill of material is going to be very vague.

That is just the first half of the equation for determining the thought process behind the pricing being used. The second half is how the price was set. When managers look at the pricing on deals, they should ask questions like this:

> How did you come up with the price to use on this deal?
>
> What competitive intelligence have you used in setting the price?
>
> How do you think that the competition is going to react to this price after the first bid? What is your plan to adjust to or outflank that reaction?

Far too often, the first price on a proposal is based on a cost-up model and has nothing to do with what the competitive situation or the budget needs of the customer are. The salesperson should be able to walk you through this very clearly. If this isn't the case, it's a major red flag.

Compelling Value Proposition

> Why should the customer want to do this deal with us?

It's a basic question to be sure, but if the salesperson can't give you a clear and concise answer to it right away, then the deal is probably not very real. Even if the answer is just price, at least the salesperson knows the basis on which he or she is dealing with the customer in the negotiations.

Project Timing for the Customer

When you look at your pipeline, how many deals are set up with the close date in the last week of the period? That should set off the same kind of alarm bells as round-numbered deal amounts. Customers rarely set up their project plans that way. The questioning to draw this out starts with a simple, open-ended query:

> How did you come up with this close date?

> What conversations have you had with the customer about the project timing?

For a real deal, the salesperson should know what the customer's timeline is and should have worked backward from there based on your lead times to design, approve, and produce the product or service.

The salesperson would use this to drive the real-world deadline that the customer would have to close the deal in order to meet the timetable. When someone walks the customer through that, then the customer will share the same view of the deadlines to get an order placed.

Knowledge of Competitive Landscape

> Who is your competition on this deal?

Stupid question? Maybe. But how scared are you if you look at your salesperson's face when you ask this and see the same look as a deer in the headlights?

Once they have gotten past the preliminary stages of a deal, a salesperson should always be able to lay out who the competition is, give a brutally frank assessment of where you stand in relation to competitors, and list the actions that have been and are being taken with the customer to put him or herself in the best position to win.

By the way, sometimes the toughest competition is not another company at all; it's something that I like to call "do nothing." There is an old maxim that "If it ain't broke, don't fix it," and for companies in the press of doing their day-to-day business, the simplest decision can be to just kick things down the road a bit—particularly when there are budget issues.

The only real defense that salespeople have against this is to be sure that they have compelling value propositions that the customers really understand.

Please keep in mind the intent of all of these questions—it's not to make the salesperson feel like their manager is beating them up or questioning their competence. As we have discussed many times, what we are really trying to give to our salespeople is focus.

A properly conducted series of coaching sessions on salespeople's pipelines is not only going to help them to clean out the junk deals that are just going to distract them, but it is also going to train them on how to self-edit in the future. Cleaning the pipeline is not an event; it has to be a continuous process.

Once the pipeline is clean, we can really start to view it in a way that has more meaning to the salesperson and with a clear set of definitions that everyone in the organization uses in the same way. This is one of those things that seems really stupid and basic until you start checking around.

Test this for yourself by taking just a few minutes to run an experiment. Using whatever terminology that you use for forecasting, call five people in your sales organization, and ask them to define the terms. You might be surprised at the range of answers that you get. I know that I was.

The first step to getting your forecast straight is to be clear on how you define the various stages and forecast categories that deals are in. I can't tell you how many variations I have seen on this. Many of the variations are fine, but too many of the systems that I have seen suffer from two problems: too many discrete stages or forecast categories and too much vagueness about what separates each one from the others.

One decent test for this is the need for "help" screens in your CRM tool. If you have to have them for deal stages or forecast categories, then your process is too complicated.

Deal stages are designations of the various milestones that salespeople are going to hit as they advance deals toward closure. Most of the leading CRM tools use a common set of terms to denote those stages but have fairly vague definitions for those stages. When the definitions are functional, there is less chance of misinterpretation.

Here is a fairly common set of deal stages along with that kind of functional definitions:

> **Prospecting**: The salesperson knows that the opportunity exists and is starting to investigate it.
>
> **Qualification**: The salesperson is figuring out what the customer really needs and is determining the initial scope of the deal. The salesperson is also trying to identify the true decision makers and what the central value proposition to the customer will be.
>
> **Quotation**: The salesperson and the sales-support teams are generating the formal proposal or bill or material and setting the initial price.
>
> **Negotiation**: The customer has narrowed the choice to the final few (or only) bidders and negotiations to a final price, and terms are underway.

Closed Won: The deal is won, and the purchase order is in hand.

Closed Lost: The purchase order or contract is in hand with a competitor, or the customer has officially canceled the project.

I've never been comfortable with the use of the prospecting or qualification stages in forecasts or calculations of the total value of a pipeline as these stages can grossly inflate the overall pipeline. You know so little about these deals that by definition the values used and the timing of the deals is really more of a guess. It can be best to either set the values of all prospecting or qualification deals to one dollar in value or automatically omit them from the overall forecast and any summation of total pipeline.

The total value of the pipeline should only be based on the deals in the quotation and negotiation stages.

Many of the systems out there—as well as the standard settings from most CRM providers—tend to break down what we call the qualification stage into several sub-stages. My issue with that approach is that these tasks are hardly sequential, and wherever a salesperson is showing the deal through those phases will vary significantly from salesperson to salesperson. The stages just don't tie to the functional way that salespeople work.

As a rule, the simpler that you can keep all of this, the better your data will be.

Even with these definitions, the transition between a few of these stages can be a bit fuzzy. Moving from prospecting to qualification can be a bit of a judgment call, but you can make the definition more functional. One example would be tying it to the first meeting that the salesperson has in which the scope and timing of the deal is identified.

There can be a similar fuzziness between the quotation and negotiation stages. Again, a functional trigger is best to take any ambiguity out of the transition. One example would be to time it with when the customer has given initial feedback on all of the proposals that it has received and has made the first cut in the number of vendors being considered.

Forecast categories are classifications that we put on deals to figure out how they will each contribute to our overall path to making the number. This is one of the biggest areas where the lack of clear definitions simply kills the accuracy of forecasts. When everyone is categorizing deals differently, the aggregated data becomes almost useless.

As with sales stages, forecast categories can be classified by functional activity to minimize the amount of reinterpretation that we get.

Here is a fairly common set of forecast categories along with that kind of functional definitions:

Won: The purchase order in in hand.

Committed: The customer has told us that we will receive the order.

Best Case (Gap Close): Deals identified as having the best chance to potentially close in the quarter and close the gap to plan.

Pipeline (Pool): All remaining open deals.

This is by no means the only set of definitions that you can use. If you have historical terms or ones that match other business processes, use them. If your process works better with a few more stages or different definitions, great! Just do your best to keep them simple and clear—that help-screen test can be a good one to keep you on track.

The key is to have clear, functional definitions and to be sure that everyone is using them.

The terms that I have described here are used by most of the major CRM systems out there, but there are few that I feel confuse people with their names and some of the more common definitions used by companies in their implementations.

For example, I have seen "Committed" and "best case" are described in terms of how the salesperson "feels" about the deals. "Committed" has been defined as the salesperson committing to the manager that he or she will bring the deal home, and "best case" meaning that although it's not guaranteed, the salesperson feels that it has a chance if everything breaks the right way.

That kind of classification can make it very hard to forecast properly as it is so subjective and varies significantly in interpretation from person to person. The functional definitions that you see above are much less likely to be reinterpreted.

Let's take the "closed-won" deal stage or the "won" forecast category to start with. I can't tell you how many times I have had a quarter come up short because a "closed-won" deal was not entered. Why? Because the salesperson only had a verbal commitment and did not have a physical order that they could actually enter. It can be best to be old school on this. If you do not have the order in hand and the form or terms of it are not bookable as an order per your controllership rules, then don't count it as won.

Discipline around this is tough as all salespeople like to think that they have orders when they get a variety of positive indications, but you can't kid yourself—nothing is worse than having to back $500K out of your number the day after the period closed because the T&Cs were not approved or the purchasing agent who actually issues the order was on vacation.

"Committed" can also be a big variable. What one salesperson is willing to commit to will often have more to do with his or her comfort with risk than the probability of closure. Having a firm verbal commitment from a customer, though, is a specific thing. There is still some risk to closure from bureaucracy, but that can be managed much better than a salesperson's individual definition of their commitment to try and close it.

For "best case," I actually prefer to use a different name altogether: "gap close." Since this is the subset of deals that the salesperson is going to focus on to close the gap to plan, "gap close" is a more accurate term. There are any number of ways to determine just which deals we will give this designation to, and we will discuss them extensively later.

Finally, "pipeline" is the name that I dislike the most here. It is often confused with the overall pipeline, which is not what these deals really are. I prefer the term "pool" for this class of deals. These are the lower-probability deals that are still viable for the period and that the salesperson will be mining to find additional gap-close deals when needed.

The real art to classifying these deals is being sure that they actually are viable. The sales manager should always put due diligence into pruning this list—particularly with older deals. The coaching questions discussed earlier in this chapter can really help with that task.

The next step is to be sure that you are building up your forecast in a way that is clear to everyone involved. That means keeping it simple. One way to do this is to think of your forecast structure as a stack of relative probabilities, defined like this:

Plan: Quota for the period.

Floor: Closed + committed deals to date.

Call: Sales leaders' best current estimate of where they will end the period.

Ceiling: Closed + committed + gap-closer deals.

The central idea here is to establish a floor and a ceiling to the forecast. If you are doing this well, no matter how you end the quarter, it should always come in the range between those two numbers.

When you set the floor as based on closed and committed deals, you are telling your business that there is no way that you are going to come in below that number. You have to be careful with how people think about this number. By its very nature, it is going to start out low at the beginning of the period and move higher and higher over time as the salespeople close and get commitments on more and more deals.

Trust me, once you start using this definition, if you don't explain it properly, you will have executives' heads exploding when they see the number during the first week of the period.

When you set the ceiling, you are giving the highest level that you can hit if you close every gap-closer deal. Again, be careful how you set the expectations for this number as someone could easily think that this is a realistic number to hit—it's not. To hit the ceiling, you would have to assume that your sales team has a 100 percent closure rate on focus deals.

If you team is that good, you should be sitting on a tropical beach that you own—not reading this book. Closure rates will vary considerably from team to team and salesperson to salesperson, but a typical closure rate for a strong salesperson is one out of every three deals.

Based on this concept, early in a period, you might get a model that looks like the diagram below, which was developed with Alpine Metrics:

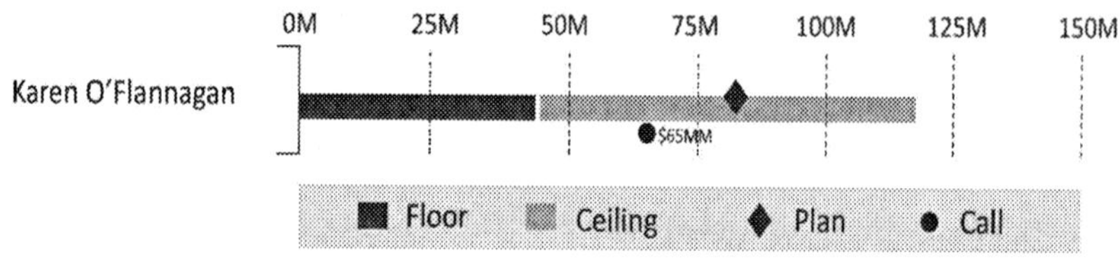

(Figure 3.2.1)

The dark bar is indicating a floor of about $40 million in closed and committed deals against a quota of $85 million, indicated by the diamond. That means that this sales manager has a gap of $35 million to close by the end of the period. The sales manager and his or her team have classified another $75 million in deals as gap closers, giving a ceiling of $115 million.

This view is one that I like the best for *see*ing where the sales team or an individual salesperson is. I like it because it shows the path that the person is going to follow as the period progresses to actually make it to the number. If the person doesn't have a path or the existing path is risky, it jumps off the page.

KEY TAKEAWAYS:

* Your pipeline needs to be continuously scrubbed through coaching sessions between the sales manager and the salesperson. Each deal should be questioned around its age, time at sales stage, clarity of the value, knowledge of the decision making, the quality of the value proposition, the understanding of the customer's timeline, and the salesperson's understanding of the competitive landscape.
* You need a common understanding of the definitions of all of your deal stages and forecast categories. The definitions should be as functional as possible to reduce misinterpretation.
* Think about your path to making plan in terms of the value of deals that are needed to close the gap between your current position and your plan.

* Build a clear view of the value of your pipeline and express it as a range—it builds from a floor made up of closed and committed deals to a ceiling made up of gap-close deals.

Chapter 3-3

Think

Once we have a clear view of our pipeline and our current forecast position, we need to be as smart as possible in determining the best deals to invest time and effort in to make our plan.

> It's a beautiful summer day in Chicago—which we get to watch through the conference-room windows as the operating committee of my unit is in day two of a week-long planning session.
>
> The room is long and narrow, and we have about fifteen people going up and down each side of a U-shaped table setup with the obligatory screen of PowerPoint death up at the front and a table of caffeinated beverages lined up at the back.
>
> As chance has it, I end up sitting next to the sales leader of the division into which we report. He is a real pro who has been around the business for decades and has been leading commercial efforts at a high level for several years. Tall, trim, square jawed—the poster child for the kind of confident leader that you expect at that level.

> As the other leaders in the unit go through their slide decks, he starts a whispered side conversation with me asking about the statistics of my team's pipeline.
>
> I give him the answers to each question, but as I try to explain the particular issues of major deal A or major deal B, he keeps going back to the numbers. How many deals are there, what is the average per salesperson, what was our average close rate last quarter?
>
> He can tell that I am having a hard time following why he doesn't want to hear about the deals themselves. He gives me kind of a wry smile and looks at me as he says, "Look, at a certain point, it's just math."

That has stuck with me for years. It finally got through to me that how you think about a pipeline varies significantly depending on the level from which you are viewing it. The higher that you go in sales leadership, you will have a more and more macro view of the numbers and the probabilities of deal closures.

As a salesperson on the front line, you have a very tactical view. The salesperson has to perpetually ask, "Which deals am I going to close to find my way to my number?"

This is where companies normally turn to whichever business-intelligence tool they are using to try and find the answer, but it's also where those tools show their limitations. Dashboards can be very sexy and cool—animated, slick graphics and voice interface—but the problem is that while a dashboard can tell you where you are, they rarely tell you *what you can or should do about it.*

That's the key question that I was referring to earlier, and it is missing from the manner in which almost every company approaches its pipeline. Now,

I am not saying that the sales leaders don't know this reflexively. They do. When someone knows that he or she is going to miss the number, the first thing that the person does is try to assess how to close the gap.

The tools themselves typically don't help the leader answer the question, and that's the core problem. Without a viable tool to help answer that question, sales managers end up relying on anecdotal knowledge of deals in the pipeline that they might go after.

The flaw in this approach is clear—you are making your decision on how to invest critical time as the period comes to a close based just on what you might have heard about on a call or seen in a list of deals in your dashboard.

This is where predictive analytics come into the equation and can fundamentally change how sales teams approach these problems. However, for this to work, the sales manager first has to hold every single individual in the team accountable to make his or her number.

Does this sound at all familiar to you? You have a sales team of ten people. On average, the team tends to make its number as a group, but every period, there is a Herculean effort to close a particular deal or to get more revenue from a particular customer or channel. When you look at the team over time, you notice that it is always the same two or three people who are making the Herculean effort.

Holding each individual accountable may sound simple, but in practice, it's not. When you get into the whirlwind of making a period, the focus of the management team turns inevitably to what is needed to close the top-ten deals. You focus on those deals instead of balancing that with your overall team members as well.

The problem with this is that those deals that you are focusing on are already in play—we are missing the ability to know which other deals we should also be bringing into play. Diving into the underperforming team members can be an important vein to mine as you look for those additional deals to bring into play.

With predictive analytics, we can view our pipeline in a way that tells us very specifically which salespeople are likely to miss their numbers and what the action plan can be for each of them to prevent that. The core principle to do this is simple: know how big a gap there is to plan, and then identify enough deals to cover that gap.

Let's go back to the example that we used at the end of the last chapter and the tool from Alpine Metrics.

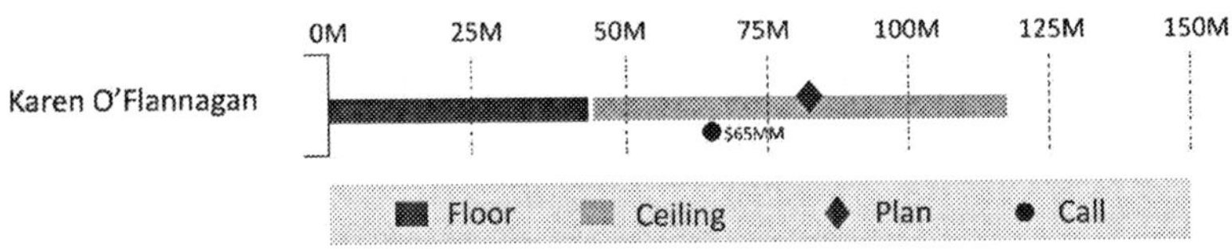

(Figure 3.3.1)

This sales manager, Karen, has a $35 million gap to her plan. If we assume that this team has a typical one-in-three close rate, then Karen has a problem.

With a $35 million gap, there should be at least $105 million in identified gap-close deals to ensure that the team can hit the quota. Because of this, Karen is saying that the forecast, or "call," is $65 million at this point in time.

For Karen to make it all the way to quota, we need to help her and her salespeople to *think* about the pipeline of deals and use predictive analytics to focus on the best deals to make the plan.

Below is an example of her team being viewed using the same Alpine Metrics forecast stack that we used for Karen.

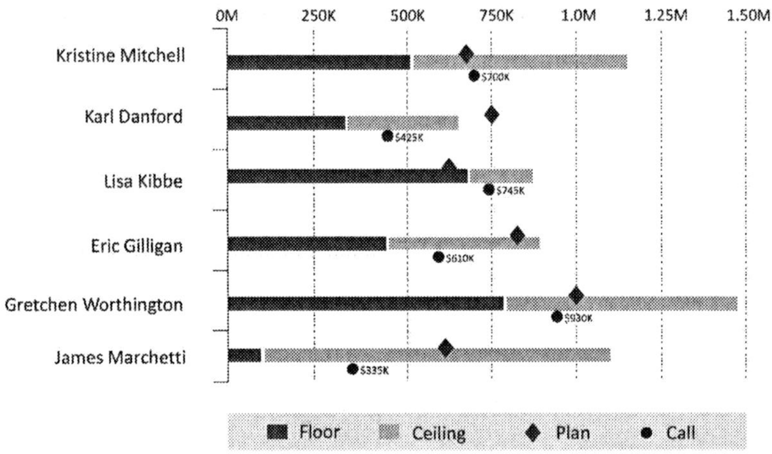

(Figure 3.3.2)

In an ideal world, we want to ensure that everyone on the team has a path well beyond plan. On this chart, that means that the diamond representing plan will be well to the left of the center of the gap-closer deals shown in the light bar for the ceiling.

At this point, the sales manager needs to do some fast triage on the team. Here is how I would interpret the data in the tool:

> Kristine and Gretchen are in the textbook position, with their diamonds for plan well to the left of center of the light bar of gap-closer deals.
>
> Karl, on the other hand, is looking at a very serious situation—even if he closes 100 percent of his gap-closer deals, he won't come close to making his plan.
>
> Lisa is in the best possible position. She is already beyond her plan, and everything else that she does is going to represent upside for her

team and, if her incentive is designed properly, significant increases to her income.

Eric is a real risk. Theoretically, he can make his plan, but he will have to close on almost every deal in his pipeline to do it.

James has two kinds of risk at the same time. The first is a timing risk. While there are lots of deals in his ceiling, a very small number have closed to date in comparison to his peers. The second risk is around close rates. While James certainly has more headroom than Eric, he still needs to close half of his deal volume to make plan.

As you get more sophisticated with this level of management, you will start to identify specific close rates for different salespeople and customize your expectations for how much gap-closer deal volume they need to have.

If Lisa has a hit rate of 50 percent on her deals, then you know that she only needs to have twice her gap to plan in gap-closer deals. If James has a hit rate of 25 percent, then you know that he needs to have four times his gap to plan in gap-closer deals.

It's rare to run a sales team in which every salesperson is making his or her number every period. What most teams need to do is simply to flip the ratio—have most people making their numbers instead of just a few.

The first step to making that happen is to hold people accountable, but key step is showing the salespeople precisely which deals in their pipelines to focus on.

We will start by figuring out just how large a population of deals are needed for each salesperson to hit the number, and then we will move into discussing the selection of just which deals to focus on.

Yet again, the key thing here is focus. The salesperson might have one hundred deals in the pipeline but can't possibly focus on that many deals. Salespeople need a process to filter those deals down to the ones that are the smartest in which to invest their time.

The salesperson only has so many selling hours to spend in the remainder of the period. The sales manager has to help the salesperson spend those selling hours on the best customers and the best deals to get a return on that investment.

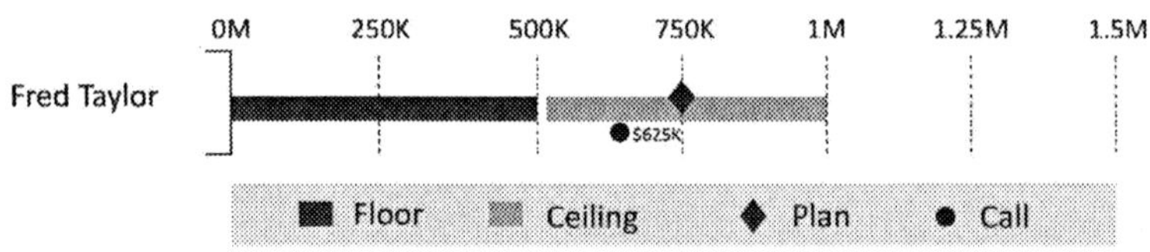

(Figure 3.3.3)

Let's think in terms of a salesperson named Fred Taylor. Fred has a plan of $750K for the period and has $500K in his floor as closed and committed, giving him a gap to plan of $250K. Fred has identified $500K of gap-close deals, giving him a ceiling of $1 million were he to close every single one those deals.

We will assume that Fred has a historical close rate of 25 percent of his deals. Based on that, with his current inventory of gap-close deals in his ceiling, you would expect him to close another $125K and finish at $625K for the period.

To get all the way to his plan, Fred needs to identify at least $1 million worth of deals to focus on for the rest of the period and then match his historical closure rate of 25 percent. The problem is that currently, Fred has only identified $500K in gap-close deals.

If a sales manager is following the methodology that we have been discussing, the normal next stop would be to just tell Fred that he needs to identify another $500K in gap-close deals. Fred would then be expected to comb through his pipeline and identify $500K in best-case deals and get to work on closing them.

That approach is certainly going to increase the chances that Fred will make his plan, but there is a limitation to it because there is not likely to be a very objective selection process between the deals in his pipeline. Fred is more likely to focus on the largest deals or the ones with the customers that he feels the most comfortable with, rather than bringing any real process to the selection of the deals.

Fred is most likely to end up burning valuable selling hours on the wrong deals.

This is where predictive analytics can come to the rescue. With predictive analytics, you can use past behaviors and history to assign real probabilities to each deal in the pipeline. The algorithms developed by Alpine Metrics are able to use this data to predict just which deals in a pipeline are most likely to close and when.

How does this work? It starts with historicizing the data in the CRM system. For Alpine Metrics, that meant that developers kept a daily series of snapshots of forty-five key data fields in the CRM over a period of time to build their data lake on deals. Surprisingly, most CRM systems do not historicize data by default—what you see in the CRM is typically just current-state data or information recorded the last time that a data field changed. This is not a regular record over time.

This kind of historical record is what is needed for the type of analysis that can detect trends and patterns. As more time passed, the Alpine Metrics algorithm could see which combinations of variables tied to the deals that were won or lost and when the deals were closed. That's a bit of a gross oversimplification of the process, but the bottom line is that once the artificial intelligence in the system had enough data to see the patterns, it could predict what would happen on a deal with a stunning degree of accuracy.

There are multiple uses for this type of information, starting with the ability to take a more sophisticated view of a salesperson's pipeline. Let's take another look at Fred's pipeline from above—but this time with the ability to both see historical information and use predictive analytics on outcomes.

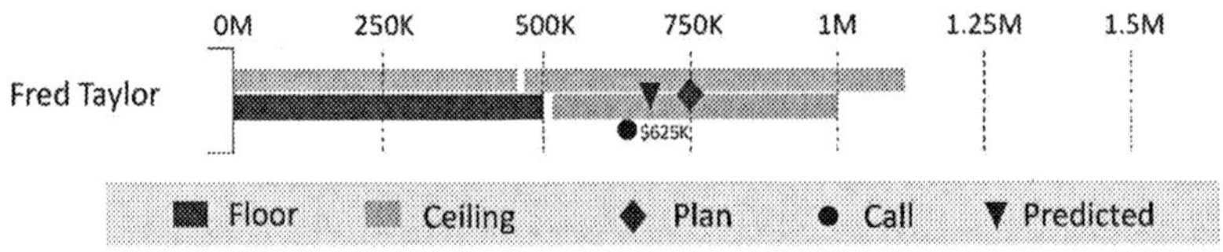

(Figure 3.3.4)

The light bars at the top represent what Fred's pipeline looked like the last time that we reviewed it. As time has gone by, you would expect that his floor would go up as more deals are closed and committed—and his has gone up slightly.

What is concerning, though, is what has happened to his ceiling. The bar for the ceiling has gone down by $100K, meaning that deals have dropped out of his gap close category without being replaced by other deals—that means that Fred's chances of making his plan are getting worse.

This may not seem like a major issue, and the amount is small enough that the manager may not notice the difference between two reviews, but it can have a significant impact on Fred's ability to make his number. If the same thing is going on with multiple salespeople on the team, the manager is going to see their projections for the quarter going down steadily without any "big" cause to point to and correct.

Making this historical change easy for the manager to see gives him or her the ability to do something about it while there is still time.

While that functionality comes from just having a historical record of the data, predictive analytics allow us to take a significant step beyond the manager's "call" on where the salesperson is going to finish the period. Systems like Alpine Metrics can look at the probabilities of each individual deal in Fred's portfolio and predict where he is currently likely to exit the quarter.

As useful as that prediction is at a strategic level, the real power of predictive analytics comes in when we apply them at the tactical level to filter the deals in the salesperson's pipeline.

Let's go back to the question that Fred had to answer above. He needs to find the deals in his pipeline that he can focus on for the best possible path to make his number. As we discussed earlier, in most salespeople's worlds, when they need to think about focusing on more deals to close gaps, they tend to just look at the largest deals.

With predictive analytics, Fred can look at his pipeline and easily see the deals that he does not already have in his forecast and what their chances of closing are. Alpine Metrics has designed their system to allow Fred to get at this data both in a mobile environment, as part of his daily routine, as well as in the traditional desktop environment, for coaching sessions with Fred's manager.

In a mobile environment, Fred can just text their virtual assistant, Claire in a dialog like this:

> Fred: "What is my predicted call for the quarter vs my quota?"
>
> Claire: "You are projected to finish at 92% of your quota. You will need another $232K to make your quota."
>
> Fred: "What is the best deal for me to focus on to make my quota?"

Claire: "The highest probability deal not forecast to close is, ABC Machinery for $257K with a deal score of 82."

For a coaching session with his manager, Fred would work with a view in his CRM like this focus-deals tool from Alpine Metrics. A tool like this allows for a more complex view of Fred's deals.

Focus Deals

Show: Above Ceiling Deals Stage: *Any*

	Deal Name	Owner	Amount	Score	Close Date
🔍	Dynasoar Flight System	Fred Taylor	$156,004	99	28-Apr-2016
🔍	Stockton WWTP – Phase 2	Fred Taylor	$120,000	98	09-Jun-2016
🔍	Pack-Tec Shrink Wrap Pilot	Fred Taylor	$100,000	98	15-May-2016
🔍	Compton Controls Q3 Pre-buy	Fred Taylor	$209,534	97	31-May-2016
🔍	Bionic Systems – Left Arm	Fred Taylor	$800,000	96	23-Jun-2016
🔍	Eldorado Gold conveyor system	Fred Taylor	$164,566	96	12-Jun-2016
🔍	Rainbow Irrigation – System Integration contract	Fred Taylor	$300,000	95	27-May-2016
🔍	Parker Industries Plant 4	Fred Taylor	$122,000	95	1-May-2016
🔍	Phoenix Booster Station	Fred Taylor	$500,000	92	15-Jun-2016

(Figure 3.3.5)

By sorting the deals by the AI algorithm's predictive deal scores, Fred can quickly identify the deals that he can focus on with the highest probability for a win. In the table above, the top five deals alone total over $500K, and all have a deal score of 96 percent or better. This might sound like the typical approach that we described earlier, but there is a critical difference—this is not the list of Fred's top deals; it is the list of his deals with the highest probability of closure in the period. That's a powerful difference.

Do his chances increase if he goes after the top seven or even ten? Absolutely! The decision needs to rest on just how much time Fred needs to ensure that the deals close—how many selling hours does he have left to invest?

This is where the sales manager's coaching becomes critical. Once the tool shows the possible deals to focus on, the sales manager should talk through each one with Fred and review his thoughts on the path to closure for each one. This not only helps to vet the final list, but it also allows the manager to act as a valuable sounding board for Fred as they talk over the closing strategy for the deals.

The sales manager has to be realistic about their expectations for these deals and approach the conversation in a coaching manner; the salesperson has to come up with the solution while the sales manager guides him or her to it. Managing that conversation is an art.

The sales manager has to be patient and draw the answers out of the salesperson with a series of coaching questions so that the salesperson ultimately voices the approach to each deal. If the sales manager just tells Fred what to do on a particular deal, he will probably do it, but he is not going to be as invested in it as if it were his own idea. A true salesperson is certainly savvy enough to work out a closing strategy for any given deal, but it can be a better and more effective strategy if the salesperson is able to collaborate with another professional with a different point of view.

What kind of coaching questions can be effective? Here are some examples:

> What do you think is motivating the customer to buy this in the first place?
>
> Who do you think is the real decision maker? How do we know that?
>
> Who else might be influencing the decision?
>
> Do we know how doing or not doing this deal impacts how this person is measured in his or her job?

Predictive analytics can also be used for filtering deals in the other direction. Think about those deals that we think that we have commitments on but don't actually have POs for yet. While we might feel really good about those deals, any seasoned salesperson knows that an order is not an order until you have it in your hands.

Let's take another look at the focus-deals tool from Alpine Metrics. This time the tool is filtered for deals in a team's "floor" that have the lowest scores from the predictive analytics AI.

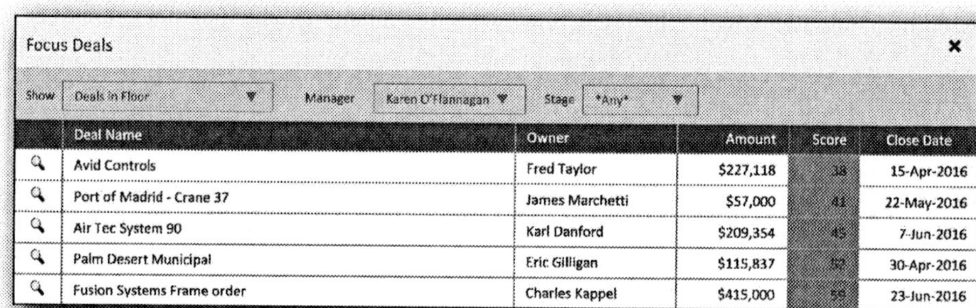
Focus Deals

Show: Deals in Floor | Manager: Karen O'Flannagan | Stage: *Any*

Deal Name	Owner	Amount	Score	Close Date
Avid Controls	Fred Taylor	$227,118	38	15-Apr-2016
Port of Madrid - Crane 37	James Marchetti	$57,000	41	22-May-2016
Air Tec System 90	Karl Danford	$209,354	45	7-Jun-2016
Palm Desert Municipal	Eric Gilligan	$115,837	52	30-Apr-2016
Fusion Systems Frame order	Charles Kappel	$415,000	59	23-Jun-2016

(Figure 3.3.6)

As you can see, the same predictive deal scores that we used to find gap-close deals can also be used to look at the committed deals in the forecast to see which of them might be at risk. If a committed deal has a score below 80 percent, it's worth taking a closer look at it just to be sure that it is secure. If it does not look like the salesperson has all the bases covered, it might be better to move it out of commit and into gap close.

As with the coaching for how to best close a deal, this is another area where skilled questioning from the sales manager can help the salesperson to see a risk that might not have been thought of already and decide on the best way to mitigate that risk.

When is the last time that you talked to the customer?

How responsive has the customer been when you have called or e-mailed him or her recently?

What is the reason the customer is telling you regarding why we don't yet have the PO?

Which details, like terms and conditions, do we still have to finalize?

What deadlines on the customer side could we use to drive a sense of urgency to place the PO before the end of our fiscal period?

In both of these cases, it is likely that questions are going to come from the salespeople around where the predictive deal scores come from. Why is the score on deal A higher or lower than that on deal B? My management teams and I have had some pretty spirited debates on the pros and cons of having the predictive-analytics tool provide this information.

One argument is that if you reveal too much about what is driving a low predictive deal score on specific deals, some salespeople who just want to get management to leave them alone will reverse engineer the algorithm and change the data in the tool to get a better score on the deal, as opposed to changing the actual behavior on the deal that is driving the low score.

The algorithm that the AI uses is based on looking at how a current deal compares to deals in the past. If the CRM-entry patterns change through someone gaming the system without chaining the underlying activities, then the ability to predict the outcome is going to degrade. The very act of knowing what drives the AI's algorithm can cause it to stop working.

On the other hand, the argument can be made that if a deal is scoring low, the salesperson is going to value the information from the tool more if it is giving the specific reason why the deal is at risk.

The answer to me is really in the middle, and depends on the degree of the information that you have the tool give about why the deal is at risk. For example, if a deal scores low because its status has not changed in some time, the tool could just give more general feedback that slow timing is impacting the deal score.

The salesperson might then realize that it has been an unusually long time since they received a verbal commitment to the deal. If it is now without a PO, the salesperson and the sales manager can decide how serious a risk this is based on what they know about the real-world situation and how the customer's logistics work, not just based on the numbers.

The main thing that this kind of approach will drive is not in-depth math exercises. What we want it to drive is meaningful and probing coaching conversations between the sales manager and the salesperson. That's the real value here—not the numbers on the dashboard.

KEY TAKEAWAYS:

* You can't accept a status quo of a team's results being driven by a small population of stars. Every salesperson on a team has to be held accountable to make his or her number.
* Once a salesperson knows their gap to plan, the best help that you can give them is to identify the highest probability set of deals to focus on to close that gap.
* Predictive analytics should also be used to identify existing deals that are actually at risk.

Chapter 3-4

Do

In David Mamet's film *Glengarry Glen Ross*, there is a scene that I think illustrates one of the biggest problems that impact the execution of deals for salespeople—the cardinal sin of just waiting for something to happen.

Jack Lemmon's character, Shelley Levene, is an older salesman, past retirement age but still needing to work to pay for his daughter's medical care. He was probably a real player earlier in his career.

Earlier in the film, we see examples of him on the phone giving very polished pitches to potential customers intended to convey his importance and sophistication.

In this scene, Shelley has just returned from a sales call on a very weak lead. He is triumphant as he has finally closed the customer and is proudly telling Al Pacino's Ricky Roma about how he closed it.

In the story, after he has made his pitch to the clients, he shows a huge amount of pride in talking about how he closed the deal by holding out a pen in front of the clients and asking them to sign.

> He then held the pen there in front of them—saying nothing—for twenty-two minutes. The client finally, in his words, "wilted" and "slumped" before taking the pen and signing it.

It's a profoundly sad moment to see someone be so proud of something so pathetic.

Why is it pathetic? Because there is no action; there is just…waiting. After committing the first cardinal sin of a "sales pitch" that was just a vomiting of information, he committed the second cardinal sin of selling: waiting for the customer to do the salesperson's job and move the deal forward. And let's face it; "wilting" is not exactly the kind of emotion that you are looking for in a customer when you close a deal.

One of my favorite books on selling is *Hope is Not a Strategy*, by Rick Page. The part that really resonated with me the first time that I read it was a discussion around salespeople being willing to spend hours putting proposals together but rarely being willing to spend ten minutes later to follow up on them. They just hope that the customers will like their proposal the best and call them with orders.

Every deal has a natural momentum, and when that momentum starts to wane, we know that we can lose that deal to our competitors. While we are hoping for the customer to call us back on the proposal, the competitor's salesperson has already called the customer for feedback and found out what it will take to close the deal.

One of the best things about a CRM system when it is enhanced with historicized data is its ability to help us see with great clarity when that momentum is being lost. With the number of deals that the typical salesperson has in the pipeline, it's almost impossible for anyone to do this in his or her head. This is another area in which we can really make CRM work for our salespeople.

Most CRMs keep track of deals in terms of various stages, as we laid out in chapter 3-2. Even if you are not using predictive analytics, the CRM should be keeping track of how long deals have been sitting at various stages.

Over time, you are going to develop a good base of experience to know how long you can reasonably expect a deal to be sitting at a particular stage. Once the deal is past that, you can tell that it is stalling and that the salesperson should be intervening.

For example, if a deal had a quotation issued thirty days ago but has not yet moved to negotiation, something is going on, and it's probably not good. It's simple to set up a report to show the salesperson all the deals in his or her pipeline that have been at a particular stage longer than the average. This does not automatically mean that there is a problem, but it's a trigger for the salesperson to look deeper, and it's the CRM that helps them to see that trigger.

More sophisticated tools like Alpine Metrics can not only show you where these thresholds are and alert you to the deals that are past them but can also use their AI to detect when the momentum of a deal is starting to slow down–before it has hit any kind of a trigger point. This allows the salesperson to take action sooner—while there is less of a loss of momentum to make up for.

If you build your system on this basis, salespeople are going to get actionable information back from the data that they have been putting into the CRM. Information that is going to help them to close more deals.

As the sales manager, you want to set up a process that inherently keeps deals moving at all times. However, just having a system like this is only going to get you so far. The rest of this is about the mind-set your salespeople have about keeping deals moving.

The best salespeople don't wait. The best salespeople always know the next step in a deal and work toward making it happen. It's that simple. When sales managers are coaching salespeople on deals or looking at one in the CRM, the next step should be the most important thing that they are looking for and helping with.

The next step is how the best salespeople move deals forward.

To do this, you need to install fields in your CRM's deals to show the "next step," the date that it will be done by, and who owns the action. This needs to be very tactical and very immediate. We are not talking about deal milestones here; those get too nebulous and drawn out. What we are talking about is the next concrete action that the salesperson needs to take to move the deal forward.

Making this work may be a major culture change in your organization. The sales managers are going to need to make the reviews of the next steps the centerpieces of their pipeline and deal reviews with their salespeople.

Just having a next step alone is not enough—it has to be the right next step. The step needs to be actionable, and it needs to be something that the *salesperson* is doing, not someone else. The salesperson can reference tasks by other people, but he or she needs to think of it in terms of how to get that person to execute.

Waiting and hoping are not next steps for us; they are openings for our competition to take the deal away. This is where smart coaching from the sales manager comes into play.

We have to recognize that sometimes it's hard for the salesperson to see just what the best next step is. This is particularly true when the salesperson has been very close to a deal for a while. The sales manager can be a great sounding board to help coach the salesperson on what the most effective next step is, as long as it is done via effective questioning.

As we discussed earlier, just telling the salesperson what to do has a limited effectiveness. If the idea for the action is coming directly from the salesperson themselves, then he or she is going to be fully invested in the idea and will drive it with intention.

The coaching questions here work best in the style of "peeling back the onion." This can be delicate. You want to challenge the salesperson without having it come off like you are shooting down ideas or playing inspector. Your role here is to help salespeople uncover new ideas.

> "So, what is the next action that you need to take to move the deal forward?"
>
> "When will you do it?"
>
> "Is there anything that you can think of that you could be doing sooner?"
>
> "When you do that, what kind of a reaction do you expect to get from the customer?"
>
> "What actions do you think that your competition is taking right now?"
>
> "What could you do to counter what your competition is doing?"

Here are some of the elements that should be in a good next step:

> It should always be a concrete action that the salesperson is going to take.
>
> It should always have a firm date associated with it.
>
> Passive items like "waiting to hear" should be thrown out immediately.

The key here is to ensure that we are creating a constant mind-set of "What is it going to take to close this deal?" It may seem trite to quote the age-old salesman's mantra of "ABC: Always Be Closing," but it is age-old for a reason.

Always having a vision of the deal-closing strategy and knowing the next step to move toward it is what separates your salespeople from the competition.

Your salespeople have to always be taking initiative, and helping them to stay in that state is one of the most valuable things that you can do for them as a sales manager. The right set of open-ended questions used while talking over the deal with the salesperson can help to drive this.

> "If we step back for a moment and look at this from the customer's point of view, what will it take to ultimately close the deal?"
>
> "What indications would make you feel comfortable that the customer will commit this order to only you?"
>
> "What issues with the terms and conditions still have to be negotiated, and what do you think will be the best way to get the customer to agree to them?"
>
> "How do you know that the sign-off process on the deal matches what you are being told?"
>
> "What is the motivation on the customer's part to place the order by the end of the period?"
>
> "What risks can you think of that could push this deal out of the period?"

These questions will work as a standard dialogue in your coaching sessions, but they can also be embedded in your CRM system to help keep track of them and maintain the focus on the agreed-upon strategy for the deal. This can be particularly important on your larger deals. You can find an example of this large-deal checklist later in the chapter.

Structured-coaching sessions like the ones discussed earlier are big parts of how we maintain deal momentum as all of the questions that we discussed above become part of those same conversations.

The idea is to have a consistent series of coaching conversations with your salespeople in which you are reviewing the pipeline, talking through the deals, and helping them to see the best paths for moving the deals forward.

This is particularly applicable when we are talking about deal momentum as the salespeople are often too close to the situation to necessarily see when the deal is stalling. Just be sure to keep the reviews regular and structured.

Beyond the questioning techniques that you can use to help your salespeople to keep deals moving, there are some specific tools that you can use as well.

<u>The 7:15</u>

Let's think about all of the things that most sales organizations ask salespeople to do:

* We have leads that need follow-up.
* We have account-plan tactics that have to be executed.
* We have the actions generated by sales calls that are now tasks to be done for the customer—they are all promises that we have made to the customer.
* We have upcoming sales calls that need to be planned.
* We have next steps on deals that have to be executed.

Now, let's do some very conservative math on a couple of these. We will assume a salesperson with a base of twenty-five active accounts, making just one sales call a day, and with twenty deals being actively worked at any given time:

* If each account plan has just four tactical objectives for a year, with twenty-five accounts, that is two tactical objectives that have to be met every week.
* Conservatively, every sales call is going to result in at least five tasks that a salesperson needs to get done for a customer. With just one sales call a day, that is twenty-five promises a week that the salesperson has to keep for his or her customers.
* By the same metric, that means that there are five sales calls to generate, confirm, and plan each week.
* If we never want a deal to go more than a week without activity, that means twenty next-step actions have to be executed each week.

That all adds up to a minimum of fifty-two key actions that a salesperson has to ensure are done—and done well—every week of the year. I don't know about you, but for me, that is a lot to keep up with.

All of the major CRM platforms allow salespeople to create tasks, assign them to themselves or others, set due dates, and then associate them with accounts or specific deals. The only issue with this is that most salespeople don't use this function.

It's likely that the salesperson is using some kind of tool to keep track of the tasks—anything from a spiral-bound notebook to task-management software—but those approaches don't tie to the CRM and don't allow you to engage the rest of the organization.

If you can get your salespeople to start doing their task management inside the CRM, they will find another one of those serendipitous places where the CRM actually gives them something back for their input.

Not only will the CRM ensure that they never drop the ball on one of their customers, it also allows them to clearly see which tasks are still pending for a particular customer or deal whenever they want to check up on it or prior to a customer meeting or phone call.

However, the real prize is the ability to engage the rest of their organization. Since the systems allow you to assign the tasks to anyone, the salesperson can assign them to tech support, engineering, sales support, or anyone that he or she is asking to engage to help the customer. As the task is linked to the customer or opportunity, the salesperson also saves a lot of typing or phone calls as all of the major details should be right there for whomever gets the task to read.

Sometimes, the commitments that we are keeping track of will even be from the customer to us, and this approach allows us to monitor those promises as well.

Just having all of this in the system does not really solve the problem though. In over thirty years of selling, I have rarely had a day in which a phone call or a natural event has not derailed my plans in some way. The natural whirlwind of daily life often forces our salespeople to be in a reactive mode.

To help your salespeople get some measure of proactivity, they have to have a regular review of all of their activity—and that leads us to what will be one of the more significant behavior changes that we need to drive, something that I have come to call "The 7:15."

The idea here is to build a behavior for a structured review that happens every day before the whirlwind starts to take over. The precise time that it is done every day is obviously not going to be the same for everyone; 7:15 a.m. is more of an illustration. The activity just has to be regular and happen before the salesperson's day gets going and the distractions begin.

The content of the 7:15 can be customized to whatever works best for you, your team, and your business model. Ideally, you can build a custom dashboard to make it simple for them to walk through this checklist while looking at the right information. Regardless of the mechanism that you set up, the flow of the 7:15 should look something like this:

Check the pipeline, and look at the top deals.
What do I need to do today to move any of the key deals forward?
What new tasks do I need to assign to myself or others for these deals?
What sales calls should I be setting up to make in the near future on these deals?
What should the plan for those sales calls be?

Check the calendar, and look at that day's sales calls.
Am I ready for the calls today?
What else do I need to get done before today's sales calls?
Do I have all of my upcoming calls scheduled and planned for the next week?
Do I need to assign any tasks to myself or others to be ready for those calls?

Check the task list.
What tasks am I behind on?
What tasks do others owe me?
What tasks will I need to do today?
No matter what happens today, what are the three things that I need to make sure get done no matter what?

Once salespeople get in the habit, this review can take fewer than fifteen minutes, but the investment of that time will pay itself back many times over.

Why? As simple as this sounds and as common sense as it is, the vast majority of salespeople (including your competitors) are not doing anything close to this.

This kind of basic structure and the regular habits that go with it are what ensure that your salespeople can be as proactive as possible and keep their deals moving forward faster than their competition.

The folks at tact.ai have built a tool that consolidates all of this information into a simple view for the salesperson to look at first thing in the morning to make the 7:15 easy to do in a mobile mode.

<u>Deal Coaching</u>

The intent of this tool is to serve both as a way to provide consistent coaching on a particular deal as well as provide some structure to the building of the overall forecast. It's a way to take the coaching dialogue that was discussed earlier in the chapter and embed it directly in the deal in your CRM.

There is real value to doing this in the CRM. By putting it there, you take all of the key information and actions that have been distilled from the conversations between the sales manager and the salesperson and communicate them to anyone else who is looking at the deal. This saves a lot of time when engaging the rest of the organization to help drive the deal forward.

Typically, the tool should be set so that only the manager can edit it, and the manager should fill it in during coaching sessions with the salesperson. The forecast-category, probability, must-win, and deal-risk answers should be a consensus between the salesperson and the sales manager.

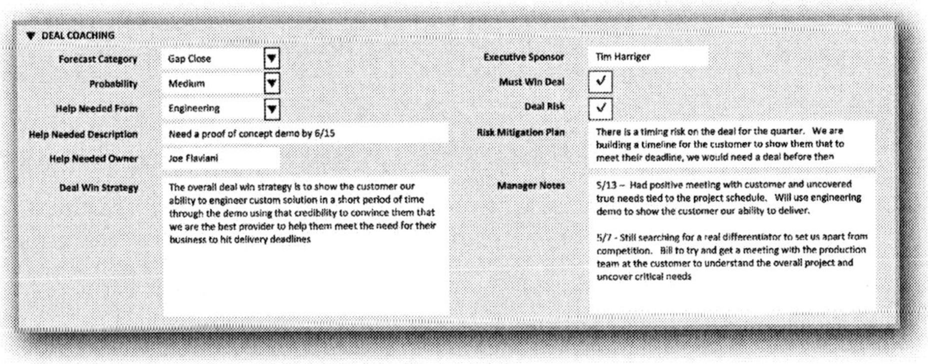

(Figure 3.4.1)

This tool allows the manager to classify the deal for forecast, probability and risk and to identify any executive level help that they want to engage. It allows them to record the agreed upon deal win strategy, risk mitigation and ongoing notes. I've found that this flows very well in ongoing coaching for large deals, but it may be overkill for most everyday deals. A simpler format that just uses forecast category, probability and manager notes has worked for me as well.

Large-Deal Checklist

The intent of this tool is the same for any checklist—ensuring that all of the basics are covered on deals. While this may seem overly rudimentary to many salespeople, it's not. When you use it, you will be amazed at how many deals you will have that are late in the selling process with critical blanks on this checklist.

While the questions here apply to any deal, you do need to decide the level of deals on which you want to use it. Personally, I tend to just use it for larger deals. Ideally, this object should be located inside of the opportunity and adjacent to the deal-coaching notes.

A report that is a compilation of answers from this checklist for all of your major deals is a useful tool for assessing forecast risk and requests for help from the organization as the quarter comes to a close.

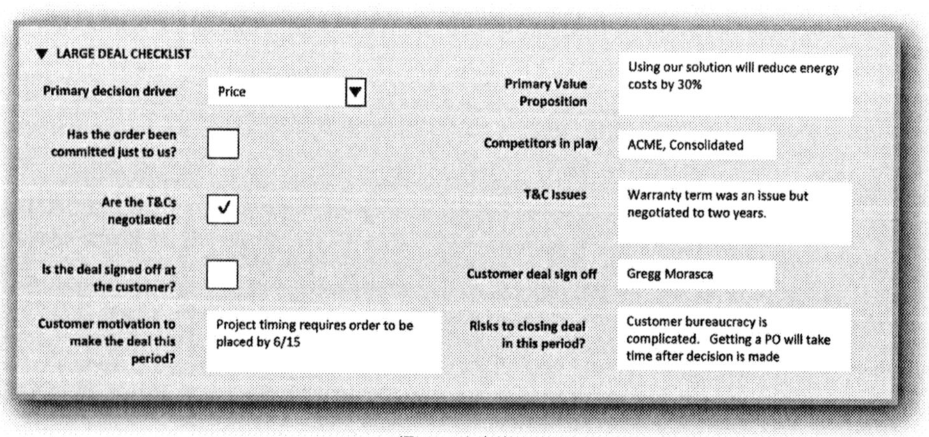
▼ LARGE DEAL CHECKLIST

Primary decision driver	Price	Primary Value Proposition	Using our solution will reduce energy costs by 30%
Has the order been committed just to us?	☐	Competitors in play	ACME, Consolidated
Are the T&Cs negotiated?	✓	T&C Issues	Warranty term was an issue but negotiated to two years.
Is the deal signed off at the customer?	☐	Customer deal sign off	Gregg Morasca
Customer motivation to make the deal this period?	Project timing requires order to be placed by 6/15	Risks to closing deal in this period?	Customer bureaucracy is complicated. Getting a PO will take time after decision is made

(Figure 3.4.2)

This checklist covers the most common issues that I have seen derail deals at the last moment. You might make a different checklist for your business, but please don't underestimate the value of having the checklist—you may be amazed at how often critical items are being overlooked until late in the sales cycle.

Support Requests

Often when a deal is stalling, it is because the salesperson has asked for help from another part of the organization, and it is not coming fast enough. One way to manage this better is to use your CRM to track those requests and their statuses.

You can do this with a function called a support request, which is described in chapter 2-6. This tool helps us in a few different ways.

> For the salesperson, it saves time in communicating the background for the request as it is simply attached to the specific deal that it applies to. It also allows the salesperson to keep track of how the request is being responded to.
>
> For the managers of the supporting organizations, the tool lets them keep track of and control the loading of tasks onto the members of their staff.
>
> For the sales managers, it allows them to see the overall view of which parts of the organization are actively engaged in moving deals forward as well as how well they are working together.

Far too often, when a salesperson is looking for help on a deal or with a customer, there is no official way for him or her to seek it out. They use their personal "secret-handshake" network to get things done.

While that may be expeditious, it is not the way to run a business. Help in those cases is going to go to the people who shout the loudest or who have the best connections and not necessarily the cases that make the most sense for the company.

By creating an organized system to bring in these requests, we get several very real benefits.

The managers of each supporting organization are able to look at each request, estimate the resources required to accomplish it, and decide on the best resource to assign. When they do the assignments, they are able to see the existing loading on their resources and both balance or reprioritize based on the customers and potential business involved.

If a business decision has to be made on approving or rejecting the request, the information needed is sitting right there with both the costs of the request and the potential business tied to it.

The salesperson and the sales manager are able to keep track of all of their requests on each organization and ensure that none of the commitments that they have made to customers are falling behind. When requests do start to fall behind or need to be reprioritized, the salesperson is able to address the issues proactively with the customer rather than waiting until the promised completion dates have come and gone.

Finally, because the request is tied directly to the account or opportunity, the salesperson and the rest of the organization save time on communications as all of the basic information about the customer or deal is right there in the opportunity to be read by anyone looking at the deal.

Key-Deal Reviews

It's one thing to ask for help that we know we need, but what about the help that nobody has thought to ask for? It's impossible for the salesperson or the sales manager to know about all of the activities in engineering, product management, or marketing that might be able to help on the deal.

Holding periodic major-deal reviews with senior staff can help to create that level of collaboration.

The idea is to gather the leaders of the key functions in the organization to review the top deals for the coming period. At a minimum, this is engineering, product management, and marketing, but it can be beneficial to have finance, legal, customer care, or other functions present. Any teams that support customers could have an impact.

The salespeople handling the top deals for the period give a brief overview, using the CRM, of the deal and the strategy for winning it. The functions then brainstorm on ways that their resources might be able to help on the deal.

Depending on your organization, this may be way outside of the box, but I highly recommend that you try it. Not only will great ideas come out of it, but it also gets the rest of the organization invested in those key deals so that others feel like they are part of the team. That can make a difference when the deal is coming down to the wire and will make a real difference in the level of collaboration in the organization.

The Deal Room

As you come to the end of the period, the list of deals that are still in play is going to get shorter and shorter, and that allows for the introduction of a practice that I like to call the "deal room."

Normally located at headquarters during the last week or two of the period, the deal room is made up of sales leadership and the key customer-care resources. The finance, legal, engineering, and product-management leaders should all be within arm's reach, along with the rest of the executive staff.

The activity of the deal room is both proactive and reactive.

The core group in the deal room is polling the sales managers and salespeople on the remaining key deals to ensure that they have everything that they need to close the deals and to suggest resources that could help them.

At the same time, the executive-leadership team is fully accessible via the deal room to respond quickly to any request or issue involved in closing a deal. The deal-room team is normally empowered to interrupt any meeting if people are needed for a decision or resources on a pending deal.

A setup like this both creates a sense of urgency and helps the broader organization to feel its role in the commercial process. Just try it once; you may be amazed at what it does to your closure rates.

Don't let your salespeople be Jack Lemmon holding a pen.

KEY TAKEAWAYS:

* Every deal has momentum, and deals are lost when that momentum wanes. The CRM is a great tool to ensure that momentum is not lost.
* Every deal should always have a concrete, actionable "next step" that the salesperson should be using to drive the deal forward.
* "The 7:15" mentality will drive daily focus of your sales team.
* Embedding deal coaching and the large-deal checklist into your CRM will bring clarity to what is needed to close each deal.
* Support requests and key-deal reviews engage the entire organization in the pursuit of deals.
* The deal room brings focused activity, timely response, and engagement of the entire organization together and will improve your closure rate at the end of any period.

Chapter 3-5

Advise

While the front-line sales leaders drive the day to day execution of the pipeline, most companies miss out on the possibilities of adding truly meaningful input from outside of that loop to add real value to the sales process. Don't get me wrong, there might be some input coming in, but is it the right kind of input?

> It was a crisp, sunny, fall afternoon on my first day at a new company as the leader of the sales team. My "guide" for the day came into my office to tell me that it was time for the sales-forecast call in the conference room next door.
>
> We got into the conference room, and the finance leader put a spreadsheet onto the projection screen while someone dialed into the conference-call system on the speakerphone.
>
> That's when I got my first surprise. As the call went live, I heard what had to be fifty beeps as various people came on to the call. I was a bit shocked as it was a relatively small organization, and I was expecting a tighter group.

> The finance leader walked through the spreadsheet, and the story it told was not particularly good. Then the fun started. The various regional sales leaders never really got to say much as different executives started to take turns berating them on the poor outlook.
>
> Their responses all tended to remind me of Kevin Bacon saying, "Thank you, sir. May I have another?" in *Animal House.*
>
> As the call went on, there really was no problem solving—what I mostly heard was how important it was for us to hit the number and that everyone needed to work harder.
>
> The call ended, and I heard another fifty beeps as people dropped off the call.
>
> No more than ten people ever did any talking.

I get why so many people wanted to be on that call—everyone wants to know what is going on—but with that many people on the call, the result is never going to be a group working to solve a problem; it's going to be theatre. To the salespeople on the line, it felt like Christians and lions in the Roman Colosseum—and they were not the lions.

Fortunately, not every call was like that. Over time, other leaders that I worked with there took more of a problem-solving approach and also limited the people on the call to the sales leaders doing the work and the resources that should help them on deals.

And that, to put it as simply as I can, is what those calls should be. Forecast calls need to feature an objective view of the numbers and then a team-based problem-solving session. They should not be beatings. Don't get me wrong here; performance issues always need to be addressed head-on. This is just not the time or place to do it.

When the forecast is coming in on or above target, the conversation should revolve around how to enhance it and how to mitigate any risks that exist to staying on track. When the forecast is coming in low, the approach has to be that the entire organization has a problem that we are all going to solve together.

If you don't take that approach, your forecasting will pay a heavy price in terms of accuracy. Time and again in situations like that, I have seen salespeople and sales managers spend the whole first part of the quarter just giving leadership the numbers that they wanted to hear. Only as things came down to the wire and reality became harder to hide did the real truth come out about the numbers.

I can't really blame the sales teams in these cases; they were not seeing any problem-solving benefit from giving an objective view early, so they took the simple path and avoided the beatings.

Clearly, that is not how any of us want to use forecasting. We want as accurate a view of where we are going to finish the period as possible. In this chapter, we are going to talk about a couple of ways to do that.

It all starts with the philosophy of solving a problem for the organization. If you can't get that change in thinking accomplished, you will always be working with a false perception of what your situation is.

In the previous chapter, we talked about how to set up forecast categories and use predictive analytics to look at how you can help individuals and teams meet their objectives for a period. In this chapter, we are going to start with how you can best build a forecast and manage it throughout the period.

The first thing that you have to do is to decide on the cadence that you are going to use for forecasting. If you want accurate and consistent information, the organization needs to plan the time to be properly prepared for each session.

Initial-Forecast View

After the end of any period, the sales team needs a bit of time to take a collective breath after the rush of getting all of the deals in that they could for that period. If you expect a perfect view of the forecast in the first week, you are really going to overload the team. That being said, by the second week of the period, it is reasonable to expect a clean pipeline and initial view of the period.

By "clean pipeline," I mean that the type of scrub that we described in chapter 3-2 has been completed, and the deals shown in the pipeline are all legitimately viable for the period. Beyond that, the bulk of the salespeople should have been able to identify enough gap close deals to give them paths to making their numbers, as discussed in chapter 3-3.

This first version is going to be far from perfect, but there are two critical things that will come out of it:

> Are there enough deals in the current pipeline to make it to the number?
>
> What are the major deals that are going to be critical to getting there?

I will reiterate again that how members of management respond to this view is going to have a big impact on the accuracy that they will get as time goes on. If the numbers are not adding up to the results that the business needs, the reaction has to be around how everyone can solve the problem together.

It's fine not to like the story being told, but the response to that has to be how everyone can engage together to find a better path.

Operating Rhythm

Properly run forecasting calls can deliver real value to the selling process, but they do take time to prepare for. If they are held too frequently, more time can be spent getting ready to report the news than is being spent on making the news.

From a frequency standpoint, during the first half of the period, every other week is normally sufficient. In the second half, weekly calls become more appropriate, and there should be some kind of daily tie off during the final week or weeks.

If there are any special commercial programs running for the period, there should be a status update on them from the marketing or product-management teams driving them during each forecasting meeting. This ensures that we are driving their actions as early in the period as possible to get the most impact.

You do want to avoid setting the expectation that the forecast meetings are the only time that help can be asked for on deals. Tactical issues should always be rolled up to the appropriate resources by sales management in real time.

While this operating-rhythm discussion is in the context of the broader organization, the same kind of rhythm should be followed by the front-line managers. For their teams, they really want to be sure that accountability is being driven to each individual, using tools like the team-summary view shown in chapter 3-1 or the Alpine Metrics forecast stack shown in chapter 3-3.

Key-Deal Reviews

In the previous chapter, we discussed the benefits of setting up key-deal reviews with the executive staff members to offer specific areas where they might help with all of the key deals. At a minimum, one of these sessions should be held during the first month of every period to allow time for those resources to help on those deals.

Although this can take an investment in executive time, there is a real advantage to holding these meetings every month. New deals likely to move into the "key" designation as you progress through the period and would be able to be addressed at that time. Holding the reviews more frequently also allows for the process to include a greater number of deals—particularly ones that might not close until future periods.

All-Hands Calls

All of the elements that we have discussed so far involve just management and a select population of salespeople who are involved in key deals. The rest of the sales team also needs to be engaged in this process, if for no other reason to see how their efforts contribute to the big picture.

The best way that I know how to do this is with all-hands calls for the sales team—with one important caveat. The content and delivery have to be good enough to keep the salespeople engaged and offer them meaningful aid. If you can't do that, you are just going to be wasting your breath while interfering with their selling time.

To make that happen, the calls have to be clear, concise, and compelling with just the information that they need and avoiding any speakers who just drone on and on. You can manage that level of crispness if you follow a basic agenda:

How are we doing so far?

What do we still need to do to hit our goals?

What new help or tools are being made available to the sales team?

What specific expectations do you have for the people on the call?

You can certainly put in some housekeeping items, but keep them to a minimum, and deliver them crisply. You should also always add recognition of specific salespeople for outstanding achievements or key deals that they closed. True salespeople are highly competitive. A little peer recognition can sometimes mean more than any bonus payment.

You can pick your own cadence, but one call a month has always worked well for me.

After you have set up your cadence, only move things around when it is absolutely necessary. Put your calendar where your mouth is. If you demonstrate how important these meetings are to you in your sales-management process, the salespeople will respect them all the more.

Now that we have covered the communication and engagement of the teams for forecasting, let's talk about how you can actually assemble the forecast itself.

It has always shocked me that most CRM systems do not natively keep historical records of your data over time. The standard CRM is really just a snapshot of your business at the current moment in time. To fully understand what is going on with your pipeline, having it historicized can help you not just to know what your current state is but what specifically changed since the last time that you looked at it.

If you don't have this done by the system, then you are relying on anecdotal knowledge from people's memories of which deals changed or dropped out since the last forecast meeting.

If your data is historicized with a tool like Alpine Metrics, you get the advantage of being able to show trends over time, and this can be a great communication tool with your teams. Cumulative-trend lines give strong visual representations of the momentum that a team or salesperson is making toward the goals. This can be far more instructive than just a table of numbers.

Here is an example of the kind of view that I am talking about:

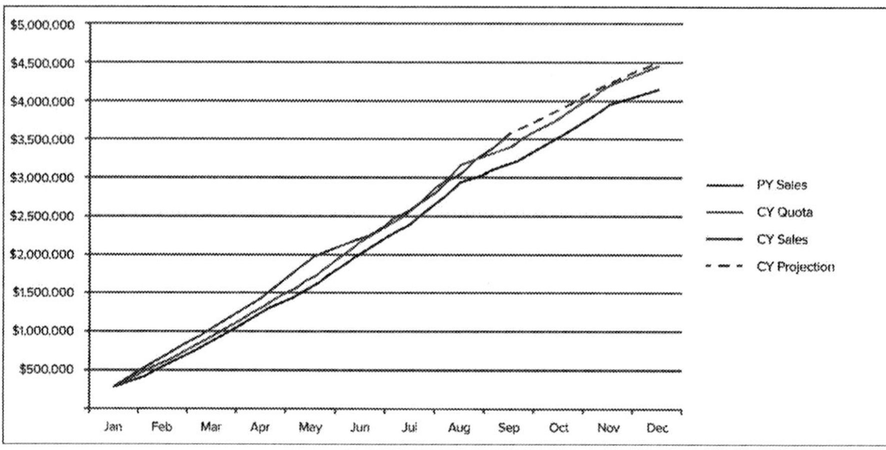

(Figure 3.5.1)

In this example, we will use a year as the period that we are working with.

The idea behind this view is simple. It gives a salesperson or sales team a clear picture of the status for the year and the trajectory for the exit. It's important that these curves are cumulative, rather than just showing month-by-month performance. By using a cumulative curve, you can see the consolidated impact of strong and weak months together.

The top line in this chart is prior-year sales. My team and I used to refer to this as the "blue line of death" because you never wanted to be below it. No matter how quotas are being built, it's very rare for them to be below the prior-year results.

The second line is the quota or plan for the current year. We always called this the "pink line of pleasure" because once you were above it, most incentive plans really started to pay off.

The third line is current-year sales—always called the "green line of good" for obvious reasons. It's the revenue that we know has come in.

Finally, we have the dotted line that is the projection of the rest of the year. There are a number of ways to generate this line. The point of all of them is to allow the salesperson to visualize how specific actions that he or she can take will change the trajectory of this line.

The simplest way to do this is to allow your system to draw this line with "what ifs" as you select different deals as being won at different times—what will that do to the curve?

A more complicated way to do it is to use predictive analytics to show the curve that results if the deals that are predicted to close happen on the dates predicted. Keep in mind, although this is more complicated, it can add truly meaningful information for the salesperson.

All of this ties back to our most essential rule for the CRM tool—it has to give the salesperson valuable information back in exchange for the data that they put into it.

If you are not ready to go to predictive analytics but are getting some kind of historicizing of your CRM data, there is another way that you can view your forecast by looking at your own historical performance in closing deals of different forecast categories.

Let's look at a hypothetical example in which we have pulled the data of our deals in each forecast category closed by the end of the period:

Forecast Category	Deals Closed
Committed	92%
Gap Close - High	65%
Gap Close - Medium	32%
Gap Close - Low	15%

(Figure 3.5.2)

This is getting a bit more sophisticated than just looking at your overall-closure rate. From this, you can build a more accurate model of how much volume you need in each forecast category to get to your overall goals.

Just be careful that your teams don't game the system for themselves. You need to keep a real discipline around putting deals into various forecast categories based on the actual states of the deals, not based on what salespeople happen to need to make their projections look good.

The calculation should be based on the dollar amounts involved in the buckets of deals. If you want to get more accurate and go by the number of deals, then I would recommend going all the way to a predictive-analytics approach, which we will discuss in more detail shortly.

You will note that even the committed closure rate is not 100 percent. Although those deals all have verbal commitments from the customer, "stuff" inevitably happens that prevents those deals from actually getting closed in time for the period. Sometimes it's the customer's bureaucracy. Sometimes it's last minute details needing to be renegotiated, and sometimes your competition gets smart and finds a way to get whoever gave you your verbal commitment overruled. Your own sales history will give you the number that matches your business.

If you want to get still more sophisticated, you can look at this same table of probabilities at different times prior to the end of the period. How did you perform on closing deals in each forecast category when you were sixty days out? How about thirty days out? Fourteen? Seven? Even if you don't make it a part of your regular process, keeping track of that information is useful and can reveal some counterintuitive patterns.

If you are able to go beyond just historicizing your data and install predictive analytics in your CRM, you can go to a whole other level of forecast. This is really the gold standard for forecasting.

In this kind of a system, every deal is giving a closure probability based on a wide array of historical-data sets. The predictive-analytics engine can look at all of your deals and just add up the ones that meet various probability thresholds.

With a system like Alpine Metrics, the longer your baseline of historicized data gets, the better the predictions are going to get. Over time, the artificial-intelligence engine gathers more and more examples of the behavior patterns of your salespeople and your customers for both won and lost deals. This will allow the AI engine to get you to a very high level of accuracy in both your deal and overall forecast predictions.

While that historical database is building up, it makes good sense to run it side by side with the above historicized system as a double check. Eventually you won't have to run both as you will come to trust the output from the predictive analytics.

Finally, we should talk about the best ways to view this data in your forecast meetings in a way that allows you to plan the tactical actions that need to be driven to get to the number. The tool for that kind of summary would look something like this:

ESTIMATES			
Quota	$ 22,000,000		
Predictive Analytics Forecast	$ 22,631,000		
Manager Forecast	$ 22,500,000		
DEAL POPULATIONS			
Forecast Category	**Value**	**# Deals**	
Closed	$ 2,100,004	94	
Commit	$ 1,210,253	71	
Gap Close - High	$ 1,215,489	30	
Gap Close - Medium	$ 1,532,123	41	
Gap Close - Low	$ 897,456	15	
KEY DEALS - PENDING			
Opportunity	**Value**	**Owner**	**Notes**
NovaCore	$ 731,840	Davis	Using NRE offer to leverage deal in the period.
Base H75	$ 286,132	Ricardo	LOI language settled, need final agreement from management.
KEY DEALS - WON SINCE LAST FORECAST			
Opportunity	**Value**	**Owner**	**Notes**
Houston Refinery 9	$ 401,853	Ivans	Order in hand last night, being entered today
KEY DEALS - MOVED OUT SINCE LAST FORECAST			
Opportunity	**Value**	**Owner**	**Notes**
Transportation Services	$ 350,000	Marks	Customer engineering cannot complete testing of the new module until June
ACTIONS			
Special discounting program being rollded out for deals that can ship by July			
ISSUES			
Need help to clear Legal / ITO Issues on 5 deals with GenDyne			
Factory having delivery issues with EL32 modules impacting multiple orders			

(Figure 3.5.3)

The idea here is to summarize the key information about the pipeline, both in terms of dollars and number of deals. The "stack" here is pretty simple – what business do you already have, what business do you know is coming, and what business do you then still need to get to make your number. You want to lay out the information as clearly as possible to show where you stand, what actions need to be taken, and what help is going to be needed.

Once you have picked the format, it's important to keep it consistent over time so that everyone knows inherently how to read it and how it all adds up. At the end of the day, if forecasting sessions are going to add any real value, they have to have that to allow everyone to focus on the right information.

This can be an object in your CRM, part of your business-intelligence dashboard, or just a spreadsheet. How you get it is not as critical as having it be a clear and concise summary of your current position. In a perfect world, all of the data fields are fed from summary reports in the CRM and your ERP system. Whichever way it is set up, it should allow the managers responsible for the forecast to edit the deals that are being highlighted and the notes, actions, and issues.

How will you know when you have this right? When the bulk of the conversation in your forecast meetings is not around the mechanisms of adding up the numbers or beating people up about performance. It's about solving the problem.

A well-run forecast meeting is about ensuring that everyone is on the same page about the current state of the forecast and how the organization is going to engage together to improve the result.

Stop kidding yourself - anything else is just Christians and lions in the Colosseum.

KEY TAKEAWAYS:

* Reacting to negative forecasting news with a group problem-solving mentality will yield the best results and drive the most accurate inputs to the forecast over the long term.
* Cumulative curves and historical-performance records will build a basic, reliable forecasting mechanism.
* Historicized data and predictive analytics will build the most accurate forecasting mechanism.

Afterword

I hope that the main idea that you take away from reading this book is that there is real benefit to shifting your company systems and managerial actions to better serve your salespeople. As a sales manager, your focus has to be on making your salespeople more proactive. If you can create any movement in that direction, then your time that you set aside to read and think about this book has been well spent.

Let me quote my friend Harvey Dunham one last time....

Where we focus, we win.

Acknowledgments

This book is dedicated to all of the true salespeople out there, working every day to make business happen.

I also need to give credit where credit is due—anything of value in this book was shamelessly stolen from outstanding salespeople or sales managers whom I have been lucky enough to work for or with over many years. To name just a few: Jack Flaherty, Bill Hughes, Scott Day, Don Leonard, Scott Walters, Harvey Dunham, Reagan Huff, James Potach, Gregg Morasca, Jeff Jervah, Brian Owens, Brad Roseberry, Tim Burns, Jim Horn, Dave Henrichs, and Andy Gravitt.

Major thanks are due to my friends who took the time to read the manuscript and offer valuable feedback—Jamie Whitcomb, Ashleigh Baker, Buz Weas, Luis Cifuentes, and the incredible proofreading from Jordan at CreateSpace.

Not a word of this would ever have been written without my mother Helen Forsgard, who dedicated her life to teaching the reading and writing of the English language. She taught me to write more better.

I have to thank my son, Alex, for continuing to put up with my delusions of having a sense of humor as I embarrass him in front of his friends and generally drive him nuts. As he well knows, it builds character.

More than anything, I have to thank my wife, Susan, for her unflagging support and love—not just while I wrote this book but also during the many years that I have spent on the road doing what I love and learning the lessons that fill this book.